Sex Spells

Important Note

The old-fashioned remedies in this book are historical references used
for teaching purposes only. The contents are not meant to diagnose, treat,
prescribe, or substitute consultation with a licensed healthcare professional.
Please use herbs with care and check with a medical professional before using
or applying any herbs. The publisher and author assume no responsibility for
injuries occuring as a result of following the instructions in this book.

Warning: This book contains sexually explicit material

Sex Spells

The Magical Path to Erotic Bliss

Stella Damiana

Michael O'Mara Books Ltd

First published in Great Britain in 2006 by
Michael O'Mara Books Ltd
9 Lion Yard, Tremadoc Road, London SW4 7NQ

A CIP catalogue record for this book is available from the British Library.

ISBN (10 digit): 1-84317-197-X
ISBN (13 digit): 978-1-84317-197-3

1 3 5 7 9 10 8 6 4 2

www.mombooks.com
Designed and typeset by Button PLC
Printed and bound in Italy by L.E.G.O.

Contents

An
Introduction
to the
Magical
Arts of
the *Erotic*

Chapter 1

*S*ex, essential to survival, has since time immemorial been a central concern of humans – and so it is no surprise that the ancient art of magic should be so closely entwined with it. Some remnants of the magic forged in pagan times survive to this day, often hidden, passed on from generation to generation, and these include the magic relating to sex. This book will lead you through some of the techniques gathered together and used by modern pagans, witches, Wiccans and magicians, and proven by lovers throughout history – the secrets your mother should have told you, if she'd known – along with easy-to-follow guides to rituals such as creating a simple talisman or setting up a more elaborate spell.

There are two main ways that sex and spell-casting work together: the use of magic to command sex and the use of sexual energy to power a magical working. In both cases the important part is the intent, or objective, as magic used irresponsibly will probably cause a rather more negative result than originally planned!

Sex can be loving and deeply bonding or passionate and lust-fuelled, but whatever the experience the fact remains that it can be at once healing, exciting, moving and fun.

Modern people often need to take time out of their mundane daily lives to reconnect themselves with their inner divinity, the spiritual power that lives within us all. Sexual magic is one of the techniques that will enrich this bond and provide you with the tools to enhance your life in or out of the bedroom.

Why magic? Why not? Sure there are other, more prosaic methods to achieve ecstatic bliss, but why fork out for a bit of plastic gadgetry when you can harness the magical forces of the universe to change your life at a much deeper level? So read on to explore this ancient tradition that will help you find the sex life you desire...

Magick and Magic

You may have noticed in some texts the spelling of magic with a 'k'. This is used to distinguish the word from 'magic' as in stage magic, conjuring or 'legerdemain' – sleight of hand. It should be clear as you go through the book that we are not discussing stage magic, so I will dispense with the 'k' for the sake of more elegant conjugations!

How to Use Magic in Your Life

Magic is neither religion nor science. Living with magic is simply a way of relating to the universe around you. If you speak to the universe in the correct manner, it will answer back. Some people define magic as the rituals you do with altars, sacred tools, robes and so on to summon and coerce angels and demons or spirits to do your bidding. Others would say that magic is 'altering reality in accordance with will', which simply means using the power within you to change yourself and the world to how you want them to be.

There are many approaches and solutions to all the problems we face in life, and magic can certainly help with many of these, but it cannot be the total quick-fix solution to everything – a magician must use all the tools at his or her disposal, not just magic. For example, if you feel threatened and scared, it would be sensible to learn a martial art to empower yourself mentally and physically, as well as mounting a magical defence. If you really want to attract a certain someone, make sure that you do everything you can in the physical world before trying to compel that person to your side by means of supernatural forces. You must play your part: it would be quite ridiculous to invoke the Archangels to guard your car if you park it in a dark side-street and leave it unlocked. By interacting with the universe on all levels you are giving yourself the best chance to gain the result you want.

Whatever type of magic you choose, you first need to learn how to be responsible for yourself before involving others. Magic doesn't just stop at the end of the ritual. The most effective forms of magic are always those that change the person doing the working, not the world outside. For example, if you are using it to attract someone who already likes you, it will help you to move up to the next level in your relationship. But if you are using it to attract someone who doesn't even know you exist yet, you will find it

11

will work only on a very superficial level. Love can only flower on fertile soil.

As has been said many times throughout history, with power comes responsibility – magical power is no different.

Marie Laveau, one of the most magnificent of the voodoo queens of New Orleans in the 1800s, taught that although some spells, morally speaking, could be categorized as either black or white, most magic, as with everything else in life, falls into the area somewhere in-between, which she called *gris-gris*, or grey (interestingly, it's also a frenchification of the Bantu word *gree-gree*, which means 'mojo bag'). This, she reasoned, is because what may work for one person in one way may not work for another in quite the same way; in itself magic has no morality as it is an energy. The morality of a magical working is determined by the practitioner.

This demonstrates the need to check the suitability and the formulation of each spell responsibly, for each person and situation, in the same way that a cook will adapt a recipe to accommodate the season or dietary requirements. *If it doesn't feel right – don't do it.*

Initiates to magic are often taught the law of three to stress the seriousness of magical actions; this law basically says that whatever you do, whatever you send out, will come back to you with threefold intensity. Only you can decide on the objective of your actions and their karmic values, but I do believe you need to use common sense when working magic and to consider carefully what you're doing.

The Different Branches of Magic

Magic and its practitioners are hard to define in the same way that art is hard to define. Often called The Art, or The Craft, magic has many branches that can be extremely dissimilar (compare Vodoun with chaos magic, for example). However, they all share some basic features.

Which Witch?

Wiccan

One of the biggest sore points among Wiccans is the improper usage of the terms 'Wiccan' and 'Witch'. Too many people use the terms interchangeably, presuming that they both mean the same thing. They do not.

Wicca is a religion, dating from the mid-twentieth century, but based on pagan primitivism, freemasonry and Western esoteric traditions, and someone who follows that religion is called a Wiccan. It is not easy to define Wicca accurately, and not all Wiccans will define themselves the same way, but their fundamental practices include observing the eight Wiccan Sabbats (major seasonal festivals), honouring the gods and/or goddesses, and creating sacred space for rituals. Many traditional Wiccans also feel that belonging to a coven is a requirement and that those who practise their religion solitarily should not refer to themselves as Wiccan. However, this is open to debate. Typical Wiccans also practise magic, and therefore are also witches. This does not mean that all witches are necessarily Wiccans.

Witch

The practice of witchcraft is nature-based and not associated with any religion, so you can be a witch and yet also be of any religion, or none. Witchcraft could be defined as the use of the natural energies within yourself, along with the energies of herbs, stones or other elements, to make changes around you. Though the skills and gifts that are part of witchcraft can be inherited from parents or grandparents, you are not automatically a witch because your grandmother was one. The use of magic takes practice, experience and learning,

just like any other craft. (On a side note: a male witch is called a witch, not a warlock.)

Pagan

While I'm explaining terminology, it's useful to consider Paganism as well. Many people use the broad term 'Pagan' to define their spiritual path, but do not necessarily identify with a specific religion. But in fact Paganism nowadays embraces a variety of non-Christian/Jewish/ Islamic religions that are usually polytheistic (in other words, they worship more than one god) and are often nature-based. Wicca is one such Pagan religion, but there are others such as Santeria, Asatru, Shinto and Shamanism – though it should be remembered that their paths are distinct and separate from one another; they are not just different names for the same faith.

Magician

A practising magician is someone who may or not follow a religion but who

might use techniques based on sigils, talismans, amulets, languages and the Kabbalah for instance. This would include such varied groups as those who practise the Enochian magic and alchemical theories of Dr John Dee, court physician to Elizabeth I; those who follow Thelema and its magical texts; and those who practise chaos magic, the most eclectic of them all – for whom just about anything might have magical significance or power.

Shaman

In traditional societies, a shaman is a person who, usually in an altered state of consciousness, acts as an intermediary between the natural and supernatural worlds to predict and control the future, cure illness, generate miracles, and the like. Originally applied to traditional healers in societies in Siberia and Central Asia, the term now is used to refer to various kinds of healers, medicine men and women, witch doctors, mystics, priests, magicians, sorcerers, diviners, and so on, in any part of the world.

Hoodoo/Vodoun practitioners

Hoodoo and Vodoun (or Voodoo as it is commonly known) are just two examples of a family of animistic, shamanic and herbal traditions which include Gullah, Santeria, Obeah, Shango, Batuque, Candomble, Macumba and others. Many of these local traditions came about as the result of slavery: with the transportation of many Africans to the New World, the traditional witchcraft of West Africa melded with both the rituals of the indigenous peoples of the Americas and European Christianity and folk magic, giving rise to a rich and heady new blend.

Of course there are many other individuals and groups who practise magic, all of whom make their will manifest in the world around them, by whatever means. The spells contained within these pages have been gathered from all these different sources, and utilize elements from a number of different magical traditions, from ancient Celtic rituals to Vodoun charms.

Getting Started

You don't need to perform long, complex and elaborate rituals to cast a spell. Often a simple mantra, uttered

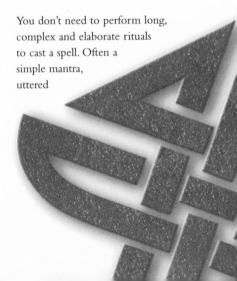

while gazing at the moon or at a burning flame, is enough to help you achieve what you desire. This book will show you a variety of methods for creating magic but it is important to remember that once you have learned the basic techniques, you can make up your own spells and they will have just as much – if not more – power.

First of all, though, you need to learn about the basic building blocks of magic.

Common Symbols

There are certain signs or objects that crop up time and time again in witchcraft, due to their heavy symbolic importance.

It is good to become familiar with these symbols before you attempt any spells: you need to understand what you're working with to fully release their power.

* The Pentagram (a five-pointed star) – symbolizes the coming together of the five elements: earth, air, water, fire, spirit; but it can also be a symbol of earth and the north for Wiccans
* The Cauldron – the womb, source of life and inspiration, the holy grail
* The Athame (a dagger/small knife, pronounced 'athamay') – the fire element in the Tarot, symbol of air and the east for Wiccans
* The Wand (a rod or stave) – the air element in the Tarot, symbol of fire and the south for Wiccans
* The Chalice (a cup) – another womb/yonic symbol (*Yoni* is the Sanskrit word for female genitalia, signifying, by extension, fertility and creativity), symbol of water and the west for Wiccans
* The Triplemoon (the waxing, full, and waning moon) – symbolizes the three forms of the Goddess: maiden, mother and crone; also the pattern of life.

Sacred Spaces

A sacred space is simply another name for the special area you will need to set aside to perform your magic rituals, and which generally includes an altar where you can keep items such as candles, incense and any tools you need for a spell. Some magicians love to have all the very best and most expensive, handcrafted items on their altars; some are even lucky enough to have a separate space to house them in. That may be important to some, but to perform most magic all you actually need are everyday items, or things that can be obtained with a little effort or by browsing on the web (I have included a list of useful suppliers and websites at the back of the book). For the most part, tools and supplies can be easily found in a decent grocery or supermarket store – after all, it is the goal or intent of the spell that is important to the spell-caster, ancient or modern, not the tools used to achieve it.

Sacred spaces are specially created places, indoors or out, where you will be able to work undisturbed, without unwanted attentions from the spirits or from your flatmate. They help to keep your spell protected until you are ready to send it out or reap its rewards. It doesn't have to be a nine-foot circle with a huge pentagram on the floor – it may just be the top of your clothes chest or your bed.

When you start, making a sacred space will involve great efforts, involving a thorough clean and tidy followed by a sage smoke smudge or cleansing which banishes negative energies. You will then need to set and consecrate your altar, which includes gathering the tools and supplies necessary for that spell, burning incense, lighting candles, calling quarters and saying prayers and evocations.

As you become more practised you will realize that this is also a way for you to prepare yourself, a way of entering into the special trance state to be at your most creative.

Experiment a little and find the ways that suit you; one of my favourite methods of creating a space is by meditation. After preparing the physical environment of the altar with music, candles and incense, visualize a small pearl-like point at the 'dan tien' area just below the navel (this is the lower dan tien, which is roughly eight centimetres below the belly button, and is the body's centre of gravity as well as being, according to Chinese medicine and martial arts, the location of your *chi*, or life force). Close your eyes, relax and breathe normally. Then imagine this point beginning to grow and shine with each breath, see all the scintillations of a real pearl until, like a bubble, this sphere has grown outside of your body until it reaches the outer limits of the space you need. Fix this space in your mind and begin your evocations.

Sage Smoke Smudging

Smudging is a ritualistic way of cleansing a space to remove any negative energies or spirits, and comes from the traditions of the Native Americans. Typically a tightly wrapped bundle of white sage is lit so that it smoulders like incense and the resulting smoke is then wafted around the space that is being cleansed.

If you use this method to cleanse your home, visualize bright light entering your space as you walk the smudge stick around the outer reaches and corners of every room. Wave the smoke into every cupboard, doorway, window-frame and entrance to your space to ensure that nothing 'lurks' in the thresholds and in-between places. After the cleansing has taken place you can call upon the spirits or a favourite deity to guard and protect your space. This method is used to prepare sacred spaces for ritual, indoors or out.

Calling Quarters/Elements

Once you have created your sacred space, you will need to consecrate it by calling on, or evoking, the help of a sympathetic deity or spirit to help your magic work and to protect you from unwanted phenomena outside the space.

Some magicians like the balance of calling on the four elements; others call on the four 'watchtowers' or the cardinal directions of the compass. Either way, you start by standing in, or in front of, your sacred space, then you breathe slowly and focus deeply, and say your chosen evocation out loud. Here is a version of the classic Wiccan evocation:

First face the east, and raise your arms over your head, visualize the Lords of the Air, and say:

'O Lords of the Watchtowers of the East,
Ye Lords of Air, I summon,
stir and call you to witness these
rites and protect this circle.'

As you do this, trace a pentagram in the air before you, and visualize playful breezes and zephyrs of the east joining you. Next face the south, and raise your arms over your head, visualize the Lords of the Fire, and say:

'O Lords of the Watchtowers of the South,
Ye Lords of Fire, I summon,
stir and call you to witness these
rites and protect this circle.'

As you do this, trace a pentagram in the air before you, and visualize flames flickering, rising and leaping in the air around your circle. Face the west, and raise your arms over your head, visualize the Lords of the Water, and say:

'O Lords of the Watchtowers of the West,
Ye Lords of Water, I summon,
stir and call you to witness these
rites and protect this circle.'

As you do this, trace a pentagram in the air before you, and visualize the mighty oceans and waters of the world, and sway in the force of the gentle swell around you. Finally face the north, and raise your arms over your head, visualize the Lords of the Earth, and say:

'O Lords of the Watchtowers of the North,
Ye Lords of Earth, I summon,
stir and call you to witness these
rites and protect this circle.'

As you do this, trace a pentagram in the air before you, and visualize your favourite landscape: wild moors, solid rocky mountains or gentle rolling hills.

Walk or trace with your wand or finger three more times around your space, noting the presence and nature of the elements as you pass. Turn to the centre and point upwards and ask the Lord of the Spirits to be with you, then point below saying, 'Spirits above me, spirits below me, spirits all around.'

Your circle, or more correctly a sphere, is now set and ready for the work to begin, with you focused and relaxed at its centre.

Evocations/Invocations

Now the sacred space is ready, you will need to call again on the help of a deity or spirit to work with you on your particular spell. (There are a few listed in the tables at the back of this book.) Find out as much as you can about the deity before you evoke it. And always treat it with respect and trust.

Many traditions command, summon, compel and order their spirits or deities to their circle – even the personal patron deities with whom a special relationship has been built. Others prefer to invite their deity to the working as though inviting a friend, albeit a rather formidable one, in a sense of mutual co-operation. Either way, evocations are simply a formal greeting, followed by the statement of request for assistance. By contrast, invocations are when we invite the spirit or deity into us so they may act directly through us; as Wiccans do when performing the Great Rite as the God and Goddess, the eternal union of man and woman.

Ending Your Spell

After you have performed your spell it is important to remember to open out the sacred space and thank all those who have helped in the working, opening the circle in the opposite direction to the way you created it; start in the centre by thanking the spirits above, below and all around.

Finally release the spirits and, as they take their leave, thank each of the lords and elements in turn for being with you:

First face the north, raise your arms over your head, visualize the Lords of the Earth, and say:

'O Lords of the Watchtowers of the North, Ye Lords of Earth, I release you and give thanks for your presence here.'

Then face the west, raise your arms over your head, visualize the Lords of the Water, and say:

*'O Lords of the Watchtowers of the West,
Ye Lords of Water, I release you and give
thanks for your presence here.'*

Next face the south, raise your arms
over your head, visualize the Lords of
the Fire, and say:

*'O Lords of the Watchtowers of
the South, Ye Lords of Fire,
I release you and give thanks for
your presence here.'*

Then face the east, raise your
arms over your head, visualize
the Lords of the Air, and say:

*'O Lords of the Watchtowers of the
East, Ye Lords of Air, I release you and
give thanks for your presence here.'*

Finish with the words, 'Spirits above
me, spirits below me, spirits all around
me till next we meet again, this circle is
now open, never broken,' to mark the
end of all magical work.

The World of Spellcraft

Chapter 2

*T*o cast a spell is to harness the elements of the life force and weave them together with your own personal power. As this life force is found in everything from rocks, trees, water, plants, winds, fire, metals, and even electricity, it is easy to think of them by reducing them to the four basic elements of Earth, Air, Fire and Water. Each part of a working is there to represent or correspond with a property of one of these elements. Add to this mixture your personal power or spirit and you have the makings of a spell. This is why the sign of the pentagram is made during many rituals – it represents the weaving together of these five powers in the manifestation of your will.

When you cast a spell you are combining these powers to create the desired result: the exact ingredients, methods and quantities give the range of subtle nuances in the results.

There are many ways in which you can make these combinations, while the type of spell depends on the demands of the situation. For example, if you are able to plan ahead, you may have weeks or months to prepare your ingredients; alternatively, it may be necessary to use creatively what is at hand. Most magicians explore and learn many methods of spell-casting, but are often repeatedly drawn to certain types of spells. Go with whatever works best for you. Here are a few of the basic types of spell that you can explore to create your own individual, tried and tested, recipe book of Sex Spells.

Candle Magic

Candle magic is not only one of the oldest and easiest methods of creating a spell, but it is particularly suited to sex magic, the flame of the burning candle evoking the element of fire, passion and sex.

There are several simple steps to preparation. If you are lucky enough to be able to make your own candles you can choose the colour, shape and size, otherwise the first step is to buy the correct candle. Some spells require small tea-light candles for a single burn, others call for a seven-knob candle (for a seven-day spell), jar candles (or novenas) with decorated glass, or ornate carved candles.

Once the candle is ritually cleansed (to rid it of any unnecessary or unwanted energies) you can then begin to charge or 'dress' your candle with the intent of your spell. The final part of the ritual is simply to light the candle, sending your desires out into the universe. Some suggestions for good candle spells follow below, after a note on how to prepare your candle.

HOW TO CLEANSE A CANDLE

⤳⤳

To cleanse a candle, make the sign of the pentagram over the candle and recite the following cleansing incantation, or other similar words of your own choice:

I call upon the spirit of the flame,
Upon the firedrakes and salamanders
Creatures of the fiery realms
And ask that you burn from this candle
Any energies that do not belong,
Let them be cast aside.
Caress and bless this candle
Sanctified with my will
By the flame which is sacred
Consecrate this candle
So mote it be!

A SPELL TO SUMMON MORE STAMINA

❧❦

This is a very effective and simple spell to summon to you and your chosen one the strength and energy you need to be able to enjoy yourselves late into the night. The candle can be prepared by one or both of you before it is required, and lit at the appropriate moment.

You will need:

❖ *1 red candle*
❖ *High John the Conqueror oil*
❖ *Sharp knife*

Method: First, cleanse your candle. Then place all the items on a cloth in the centre of your altar, and light the usual candle or candles that you keep on your altar as you begin to create your sacred space.

To dress or charge your candle, first carve a small symbol of the sun on the side, using the sharp knife. While you are doing this, imagine the energy of the sun pouring into the candle. Pour seven drops of the High John the Conqueror oil onto the fingers of your power hand (your writing hand) and anoint the candle, first from its top to the middle, then from the base to the middle, to indicate that you want the energy to be drawn into the candle. Keep thinking about drawing in the fiery, passionate, and endless energy of the sun while you are rubbing the oil into the candle and visualize it stored within it. Your candle is now ready to use.

End the ritual by opening your circle and dousing the flames of your altar candles. Ensure that nothing touches your spell candle until you need it.

When you are ready to complete your spell, put the candle in a safe place near to the bed and light it, releasing the energies you stored within, letting the warm power flow into, over and around you, powering you up for a fiery night of passion!

More Stamina

A SPELL TO DRAW THAT SPECIAL SOMEONE TO YOU

∽∾

This is another simple yet very effective spell to draw someone's thoughts to you. It can be cast on one night or over a series of nights, leading up to when you next see your intended conquest.

You will need:

❖ *1 carved red candle in the shape of a man or woman (you can buy carved candles or make your own, or a plain red one would be a suitable substitute)*
❖ *Venus oil*
❖ *Small picture of your loved one or small piece of paper with his/her name written on*

Method: Place all the items on a cloth in the centre of your altar, and light the usual altar candles as you begin to create your sacred space.

Take the male or female carved candle as appropriate to your beloved, cleanse your candle as before and place it in the centre of the altar in a holder on top of the picture of your beloved (or the piece of paper with his or her name on it).

Finally, to dress or charge your candle, take the Venus oil and anoint the candle, starting from the middle up to the top, then from the middle down to the base, to indicate that you want the energy to be sent out from the candle. Keep thinking about what you will say and do with your chosen one when you finally get together, feel the electricity that will build between you as your eyes meet, as you are drawn across the room to speak to each other, and as you leave together, laughing and flirting. Imagine the fiery passion and lust building, imagine the kisses, the caresses, and all that follows… until you both have to express yourselves immediately!

Picture that energy flowing into the candle, then when you are ready, say a prayer to Venus, and thank her for all her help. Now light the candle and send your desires out into the universe. It is preferable to leave the candle to burn down, but it is also potent if you burn the candle over a week, a few centimetres at a time.

End the ritual by opening out your magical space.

Someone Special

SEXY COUPLE
SPELL

෯෯

This spell, a slight variation on the previous one, is designed to bring a sexy sizzle back to a current relationship, reinforcing the bond between you and lessening the effects of any outside influences or distractions.

You will need:

❖ *1 carved red candle in
the shape of a couple
(a plain red one will do)*
❖ *Venus oil*
❖ *Small picture of yourself and
your partner together*

Method: Place all the items on your altar, and light the usual altar candles as you begin to create your sacred space.

Take the red candle, cleanse it as before and place it in the centre of the altar in its holder on top of the picture of the happy couple.

Then, to charge your candle, take the Venus oil and anoint the candle, from the middle up to the top, then from the middle down to the base, to indicate that you want the energy to be sent out from the candle. Think about some of the hottest sex that you and your partner have had, keep thinking about how you got together, remember the electricity as your eyes met for the first time, about how you talked for hours, kissing and teasing, laughing and playing together. Imagine all that you remember happening again as you build up the energy within you and feel it flowing out of your fingers into the candle.

31

Say a prayer to Venus, thank her for all her help, now and in the future, then light the candle and send your desires out into the universe. It is preferable to leave the candle to burn down, but it is as potent to burn the candle over a week, a few centimetres at a time (in this case it may be better to use a seven-knob candle to show that your desire is to be enflamed every single day of the week).

End the ritual by opening out the circle.

Attraction/Repulsion Spells

I am often asked what the best spell is to use if you're trying to attract the attention of someone who never seems to notice you. Should you compel them to see only you as you are, or should you make yourself more alluring to them to attract their attention? Or perhaps you are trying to escape unwanted attentions from an unsuitable admirer? Should you repulse their advances, or change or disguise yourself in some way that will make them turn away from you? If you can plan ahead, a meditation can often get to the root cause of the problem, helping you to create the most effective and appropriate spell for the situation. Alternatively, here are two simple spells that can help in either case.

WARNING: Spells for attraction or repulsion should be very carefully executed – you want to be absolutely sure you've thought through all the possible repercussions beforehand.

PULL-YOU-TO-ME
SPELL

࿐

You will need:

❖ *1 white candle*
❖ *5 tea lights*
❖ *1 mirror (preferably round)*
❖ *Dragon's Blood oil*

Method: Create your sacred space, remembering to put these items near to hand on your altar first. Place the mirror flat on the altar surface (I use a round six-inch shaving mirror) and light your usual altar candles.

Dress your white candle with a few drops of the Dragon's Blood oil to draw the energies into the candle, from the top down to the middle, and then from the base up to middle. This candle represents you and your desire, so be specific with your visualization here!

A good idea would be to focus on making it known that you would like to meet a certain someone with the intention of getting to know him or her rather more intimately if the meeting goes well...

As you dress your candle concentrate on this message and then place the candle in its holder on the middle of the upturned mirror.

Next, place the five tea lights evenly around the edges of the mirror to form the points of the pentagram. Light each in order to create the pentagram, then as you light the centre candle say the name of your desired sweetheart three times. As your energy is sent out, the light reflected within the centre of the pentagram and entwined with the sound of your voice on the aether ensures that your target will soon be unable to resist seeking you out.

End the ritual by opening out the circle.

PUSH-YOU-AWAY-FROM-ME SPELL

∂∽∾

This spell is very similar to the pull-you-to-me spell – with, however, some minor but very important changes.

Method: Create your sacred space as before. When you come to dress your candle anoint it from the middle up to the top, and then the middle down to the bottom, to show that you need the energies of the spell to flow away from you. Again you will need to be very specific with your visualization here – if you want all contact to cease permanently, visualize the target turning away from you, perhaps towards someone else. However, if you merely want a space to form between you then visualize the target just moving away, but not turning completely away from you. Meditate silently how long you want this space between you to last: you can visualize the pages turning on a calendar if that helps.

This time instead of putting the white candle in the middle of the pentagram, place it on the far side of the mirror from yourself. Light your five tea-light candles, remaining quiet. This has the effect of putting you outside the attention area of your target, however much they try to find you, for however long you have decided is necessary.

End the ritual by opening out the circle.

Oil Magic

Oils – some with a single main scent or herb, others a beguiling and intoxicating blend of the rarest and most expensive ingredients – have been used for centuries to perfume, to anoint, to preserve, and as incense. In magical practice, oils are very useful for binding certain qualities together until such times as they are needed.

There are numerous skilled blenders today who create these potent oils and luckily many sell online, so that even the most discerning spell-casters can find what they want.

Many of these oils are best created at certain times under certain conditions to increase their powerful properties. These are then used to cleanse, bless or consecrate people or objects, or they are used in baths, as incense, or to write with.

Most oils contain small amounts of the ingredients extracted from their source by various means, and are mixed into a neutral carrier oil such as apricot kernel, almond or soya oils, which can then be used on the skin; others are much more potent and are used exclusively in burners. So do make sure you know which are which, as allergic reactions are not very sexy!

Self-Anointing

Although you can choose the deity you wish to work with in your magic practice, you may find yourself being drawn repeatedly to one god or goddess, in which case it may be they have selected you! If you find that you have been chosen by a patron deity it is a good idea to find which herbs or spices are sacred to that particular deity and try to obtain an oil made up of these – or create it yourself by adding a pinch of herbs or a few drops of concentrate into a base oil such as almond or soya oil. You can then anoint yourself with this oil by dabbing a drop onto your wrists, throat and the middle of your forehead (or 'third eye' area). If the oil has a specific scent it will help to strengthen the connection to your patron deity every time you open your circle up to ask for their help. It is a sign of respect to anoint yourself in this way and helps to reinforce the bonds with the deities or spirits with which you work.

Herb Magic

Herb magic can be really effective and is so easy. As with candle magic you will be creating a combination of herbs to represent your desires according to the magical correspondences attributed to each plant. You can use fresh or dried herbs, the leaf, flower, root or bark, to prepare an array of teas, ointments, concoctions, decoctions, soaps, syrups, conserves, tinctures, medicine bags…and so on!

If you are lucky enough to have your own yard, or even just a window box, to cultivate your witch's garden, you can nurture from seed all the plants you need. You can then harvest and gather the plants at the correct time depending on the season and on the purpose of your spell; for general use most would recommend harvesting on a full moon so as to gather as much power in your plants as possible, before hanging them to dry slowly. Otherwise, fresh or dried herbs from the local shops will do just fine – just remember to perform a gentle cleansing to strip away any unnecessary energies that have attached themselves to the plants since their gathering. To do this, simply wash the herbs carefully in water, place them on your altar and focus quietly on them, calling upon the spirit of the plant to come alive again and to release its latent energy.

Here is a small collection of simple but powerful recipes for herbal teas and spell bags, for the most part using common kitchen herbs.

Teas

Teas are a wonderful way to practise
magic as they can be prepared in
advance or on the spot, and there is no
end to the variety that can be blended
– certainly enough to cover any
situation, and all from your regular
kitchen supply. Herbs can be plucked
fresh from the garden or used dried
from the store cupboard and are always
best used in a teapot so they have room
to move around, transferring all their
lovely qualities to your brew. When you
stir your tea, visualize the energy of the
plants combining with your own
wishes, wait for it to steep for a few
minutes, then quietly sip it – and your
spell is complete.

Some herbs and spices are not easily
crushed so don't be afraid to use a
coffee-bean grinder in addition to,
or instead of, your pestle and mortar.
If our grandmothers had had electric
mills I'm sure they would have used
them! And according to the
technopagans most electric mills also
spin in a deosil (sunwise) direction,
thus adding many more revolutions of
power to your intent.

SENSUALITY TEA

⁊ᴄᴄᴈ

This is a recipe for a herbal tea that Mexican women have been using for centuries and have found helps them to relax and loosen their inhibitions, and is therefore particularly beloved of newlyweds! The aromatic leaves of the damiana shrub, found in hot, dry countries in places such as Central America, are dried and used in herbal medicines, teas or liqueurs, or even smoked.

You will need:

❖ *2 heaped tablespoons
damiana leaves*

Method: Take the dried damiana leaves and steep them in boiling water for five minutes. Say a prayer to your favourite love goddess over the tea. Cool, strain, and drink one hour before retiring to the bedroom.

Use this drink over a period of two weeks for the best results, but do not use continually as a build-up within the body may be harmful.

VENUS LOVING
TEA

⊱◈⊰

This is a great recipe to enhance your lovemaking.

You will need:

* ❖ *3 star anise 'stars'*
* ❖ *1 tablespoon rosemary*
* ❖ *Pinch rose petals*
* ❖ *Pinch violet petals*
* ❖ *1 teaspoon damiana*
* ❖ *1 tablespoon mint*
* ❖ *1 teaspoon powdered ginseng*
* ❖ *1 teaspoon powdered ginger*
* ❖ *1 tablespoon thyme*

Method: Blend together all the ingredients in a pestle and mortar, stirring in a clockwise direction for a positive outcome, and visualize you and your sweetheart making love bathed in hot pink light. When all the ingredients are sufficiently crushed put them into a teapot, and top up with boiling water. Stir the brew in a sunwise direction, again visualizing your lustful intentions, then say these words:

Earth and Air,
Fire and Water,
Venus, hear our plea:
Bring hot loving
To us this night!
So mote it be.

Sweeten with honey to taste, and each drink a cup of the tea. Feel the passions begin to flame!

A tea for improving sexual performance

The use of tulsi seeds (a type of basil, and sacred to Lord Vishnu) in combination with the dried leaves of patchouli is common among the mountain people of India. It is believed that drinking a tea brewed from the two herbs, or smoking the combination through a pipe, helps improve vitality and sexual performance, as well as protecting the soul from ill spirits. Patchouli, with its pungent scent, is widely used in the perfume and cosmetics industries, but also has a long history as an aphrodisiac and a stimulant. The powdered tulsi seeds can also be used alone as a sex tonic.

APHRODITE BLEND

∂∞∽

This is an alternative blend to achieve the same result as the Venus Loving Tea. For this variation, you will need:

❖ *Pinch rosemary*
❖ *Pinch thyme*
❖ *Pinch coriander*
❖ *Pinch mint*
❖ *Slice of lemon*
❖ *Sprinkle of cinnamon*
❖ *Sprinkle of nutmeg*

Method: As above, with the dedication addressed to the Goddess of Love by her Greek name of Aphrodite

Magical Sachets/ Mojo Bags

These little spell bags combine herbs and other items in a magical mix and are carried in a charged bag, typically worn under a person's clothes. Versions of these bags are used in many traditions as diverse as European folk magic, Caribbean Vodoun, African American hoodoo, Native American medicine and Native Australian love/sex magics. The bags can also be sewn into the clothes, placed in a specific position or hung over the tap of a running bath.

They traditionally help to protect against mischievous spirits, ward off the evil eye, and offer good luck and enhanced power. The colour of the bag generally denotes the type of spell, but can be used to signify the powers invoked, the day of the week or any other correspondence (see the correspondence tables at the back of the book for more on the significance of colours). The contents can be combined from crystals, herbs, powders or any other objects of significance to the spell caster.

To Make a Mojo Bag

Take a piece of material and cut an oblong twice as long as it is wide, so that if you fold it in half you make a square large enough to hold the objects you wish to enclose.

Fold over the two short ends with enough room to allow a cord or ribbon to pass through and sew across; then keeping these hemmed ends on the outside, fold the whole piece in half and sew the two sides together.

Turn your bag right side out so that all the sewing is on the inside and thread the ribbon or cord through the hemmed sides: you now have your spell bag ready for use.

A RECIPE FOR A CLEANSING MOJO BAG

⨮⨭

Cleansing yourself spiritually is a vital task when spell-casting because it helps to mark the end of any previous workings, before you start anything else. This ensures that any residual energies are grounded and not carried through into your next working. One of the easiest ways to perform a ritual cleansing is to take a bath using your favourite herbs in the form of a soap or in a spell bag as described below. The bathtub is also significant magically as floating in a body of water symbolizes the 'in-between', a place of transition, and is also symbolic of the womb of the Goddess, the place of all beginnings and transformations. Water stands for the 'other', the dream world... so it is easy to see that some of your strongest magic can be performed while stretched out in your personal 'Water Temple'!

42

You will need:

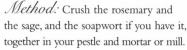

* 1 teaspoon rosemary
* 1 teaspoon sage
* 1 tablespoon soapwort (optional)
* Pestle and mortar
* Green ribbon or cord
* Green or white gauzy material
* Needle and thread

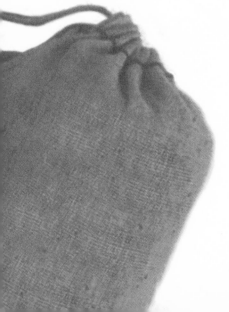

Method: Crush the rosemary and the sage, and the soapwort if you have it, together in your pestle and mortar or mill.

As you gently grind the herbs, visualize their energies coming to life combining with a gentle white light that eases all unnecessary energies out into the aether. (At this point you can also call on the assistance of an appropriate spirit or deity – for instance if preparing yourself for an evening liaison you could call upon Hathor, Egyptian goddess of the erotic arts, to energize the herbs to add extra glamour to your beautification efforts.)

Add the mix to the spell bag and draw the cord shut. Hang this bag over the tap as you run a bath. The energy of the herbs will run into the water, and as you soak yourself all excess energies will be washed away and you will be re-energized for your next workings.

DREAM PILLOW

❧❦❧

If you are starting a new relationship and feel unsure about how to take it to the next level, it is quite usual to ask the gods for a little guidance, to inspire and show you the possible paths you could take. As you often already know the answers deep down but just find it hard to recognize them, or admit them to yourself, it is easiest to seek these answers in dreams with the help of Morpheus, god of dreams and night desires.

You will need:

* Poppies (sacred to Morpheus)
* Lavender flowers
* Rosemary leaves and/or flowers
* Basil leaves
* Camomile flowers
* Jasmine flowers
* Unbleached cotton or muslin bag
* 1 glass absinthe or other strong liqueur
* A small notebook and pencil

Method: Before going to bed, mix equal amounts of the leaves and flowers in a large ceramic bowl using your fingers, crushing them to release the scents but gently so as not to powder them, all the while thinking about your question.

Take it to the Next Level

Place the bowl in the middle of your sacred altar space, and light a small dark candle.

Drink the absinthe (as laudanum is no longer available!), then meditate on the flame, chanting or humming for a while until you feel completely calm.

Offer the flower and leaf mixture to Morpheus and invite him to visit your dreams, to tease out the threads of truth, but only to show you the true object of your sexual desires.

Next pack the herbs into the small bag, sew it up tightly and place it under your pillow. Put the notebook and pencil next to your bed and then go to sleep.

The moment you wake in the morning try to remember your dreams fully and write them down: Morpheus has been known to bring very lucid dreams, but they fade very fast.

Cord Magic

Cord or Knot Magic is one of the simplest techniques to master and has the advantage that it can be done almost anywhere, as it involves no complicated ingredients or preparations.

The general preparation consists of choosing the colour of the cord as appropriate – unbleached is fine for general work, red or pink works well for sex or love magic. The cord then needs to be dedicated to your chosen deity, as you will be doing magic in their name. The cord is infused with a spell, which is either unleashed as the knot is untied at the pertinent moment, or fixed forever if the cord is burned or buried.

A knotted 'Witch's Ladder' is a traditional way of forming a supercharged 'battery' of power ready for use at any time, but when prepared for a specific purpose over time is one of the most effective tools in your magical kit. These ladders can have as many knots as you need.

LOVERS' LADDER SPELL

&~&

This spell will bring you and your partner great expertise in the loving arts.

You will need:

❖ *50 cm red cord (red food dye works well on unbleached string)*
❖ *fireproof cauldron or large cooking pot*
❖ *some cake and wine*

Method: Light your altar candles, consecrate your sacred space and take up your cord, one end in each hand. Evoke Dionysus and his consort Aphrodite, the Lord and Lady of the wild hunt and wanton love, give enthusiastic thanks and praise for their presence, feel their energy flow into your left hand, into your body and on through to your right hand, along into the cord. Tie the knots in this order:

1__3__5__7__9__8__6__4__2

(Starting at the left end, then the right end, and alternate left and right until you tie the last knot in the middle.) As you tie each knot speak the corresponding phrases:

> *Knot one my spell has begun*
> *Knot two my intent is true*
> *Knot three good loving to me*
> *Knot four teach me more*
> *Knot five the spell comes alive*
> *Knot six floating in bliss*
> *Knot seven for all I'm given*
> *Knot eight for nights of delight*
> *Knot nine I'll be sexually sublime!*

Ground yourself by eating cakes and sipping wine; and, thanking the Goddess and God, open your circle.

If you want to retain the gifts you have asked for, you must now burn the cord in the cauldron, so the knots can never be undone. Gather the ashes when cool then spread them to the four winds. (Alternatively, if you want to use the power in the knots on a specific occasion, store the cord on your altar, and when you feel the need to use it untie the knots in the reverse order to unleash the energy into the aether. Before you untie the last knot, concentrate intensely on the purpose of the cord. Focus and pay special attention to the desired outcome. Then release the knot and imagine the energy of the Lord and Lady's wisdom flowing through you.)

The ancient Greeks believed that knots were imbued with magical powers, and could stop the flow of blood, for example. Greek myths tell stories of sailors who can call up the wind by undoing knots on board ship.

DRAW TOGETHER
SPELL

ख∽ড

This is a knot magic variation
of the pull-you-to-me spell
described earlier, so again the
same caution should be used in
exercising this powerful ritual.

You will need:

❖ *3 lengths of cord,*
   string or yarn

Method: Take two cords or lengths
of string or yarn in the colours which
stand for you and your sweetheart, and
a third, red, one to symbolize your
physical relationship. Knot one end of
the three cords together to represent
yourself, then plait the cords until you
reach the other end. Knot that end to
represent the one you love. Visualize the
two of you coming together as one and
knot the centre of the plait. Finally tie
the braid around your wrist, ankle or
neck with three knots. The spell is
complete when you notice that the
plait has fallen off, sending your desires
into the universe, bringing you
together with your beloved.

The *tzitzith*, the tassels or fringes on the four corners of the Jewish tallith or prayer shawl, may well be a survival of string magic, since they are wrapped and knotted in a certain pattern involving uneven numbers, and must be spun of white virgin wool. Coincidentally, the headscarf frequently worn in Arab nations also has knotted tassels at each of its four corners

Amulets and Charms

Amulets are manmade or natural objects that are carried about or placed at a crossing or threshold either to guard against danger or to give reassurance of a direct link to higher powers. They can be obvious objects such as rabbits' feet for luck on a keyring, a lucky horseshoe, birthdate gem stones or a *mezuzah* on the

doorpost, or, less obviously, a piece of red string on the wrist, a stone carried in a pouch or an intricately carved brooch.

There are of course amulets to draw sexual prowess to the wearer, but although ancient Roman and more recent Thai and Hindu penis or lingam amulets abound, depictions of the vulva or *yoni* are relatively uncommon. There are two reasons for this: first, the female figure as a whole has been the object of worship as in the famous Sheela-Na-Gig images of Ireland. Second, the subtle folds of the female genitals are more difficult to render than are the bold cylinder-and-spheres of the penis and testicles, so more often a seashell image is substituted.

LOVERS' AMULETS

❧❦❧

When you exchange small gifts and tokens with your sweetheart, you can magically charge them to create an extra special gift to strengthen the bonds between you. These amulets can be anything of significance to you, whether, for example, pebbles found on a beach or items of jewellery (an ankh, which depicts the union of male and female, or a pentacle, which has been used as a protection against negative influences and to symbolize positive power, working with the five elements of nature). To charge them, you will need:

❖ *Your chosen amulets*
❖ *2 bowls of water*
❖ *Pinch lavender flowers*
❖ *Pinch rosemary leaves*

Method: Working in your sacred space, take one of the bowls of water and add the herbs. Place your amulets into the other bowl of plain water and start to visualize the cleansing properties of the water working, while uttering these, or similar, words:

Three times I cleanse these amulets
So these two remain as one.

Transfer the amulets to the bowl with the herbs and visualize you and your partner wearing the amulets, kissing each other deeply as the amulets pulse with power. As you imagine this, recite the following words:

Three times I call upon you, erotic Eros.
Eros! Rain down your blessings.
Eros! Teach us the ways of love.
Eros! Unite us in bliss
With every single kiss.

Finish the working by opening out your sacred circle.

Your amulets now form a bond with each other and you, and empower you with all the loving arts of Eros to call upon whenever you get together – enjoy them to your hearts' desire!

You can also use charged amulets to safeguard your partner by evoking the protection of a specific deity to the wearer of the amulet.

Talismans

Amulets, charms and talismans are very closely related in the way that they work but talismans differ by the fact that they are made for a specific purpose by magical means. The sole purpose of a talisman is to attract benefits and rewards to the wearer, and most involve the use of arcane language and symbols to invoke or compel the aid of powers such as angels, elementals or deities. Some take sacred geometrical forms, such as mandalas, pentagrams, hexagrams and spirals. Others consist of simple stones with rudimentary symbols scratched onto them, possibly with a hole for a cord to pass through so that it can be worn about the body. Some of the earliest artefacts of human civilization are talismans such as these.

In medieval times sorcerers would etch complex designs on parchment or flat pieces of metal, which would be worn as amulets. The designs were usually taken from grimoires, or spellbooks, which contained what were claimed to be ancient esoteric secrets, often derived from Jewish/Christian demonology. Today talismans survive in the form of medals (St Christopher medals for the traveller, for example), saints' relics, small carved objects depicting symbols, whether Hindu,

Taoist, Buddhist or other, or lucky charms or even tattooed depictions of such symbols as mandalas, yin-yang or I-Ching hexes.

Sigils

Sigils are simply pictorial representations of a spell. Medieval magicians would use numerology to translate the words of their desires into numbers, then would pick out the numbers on a magical square and receive their power symbol by tracing out the shape that resulted when the numbers were joined up. Modern sigils start with words which are then transformed into pictures and magically charged. A sigil will contain the totality of your intent, and is especially useful when you cannot speak your spell out loud.

SEXY SIGIL SPELL

ৰ্জন্তক

This is a useful way of using you and your partner's combined sexual energy to help you solve a problem you may face in your life (whether sex-related or otherwise).

You will need:

❖ *Pen and paper*
❖ *A willing partner*

Method: After a meditation or grounding in your sacred space you need first to decide what you wish your magic to achieve. Do you want to seek answers to a question, seek guidance or physically manifest a certain situation? Whatever you decide, start writing down what you are aiming to achieve, everything that seems to just pop into your head.

When you are content that you have written down everything you need to, start crossing out any duplicated words. (Obviously this is easier to do if you have been writing short and pithy comments, but do not let that influence you: the spell will be more potent if you have disclosed all.) When you have reduced all the duplicated words, start deleting duplicate letters.

When you are left with your final reduction, take a fresh sheet of paper and copy over the final collection of letters. Then take another sheet of paper and draw one of the letters large in the middle of the page. One by one

combine all the other letters inside and around this symbol. They can be turned on their side, upside down, back to front or however the fancy takes you, until you are happy with your symbol. At first it may take you a few tries to be comfortable converting letters to images, but with practice this process can flow much more freely.

Now trace your spell sigil out onto a fresh piece of paper and put it onto your altar. Modern sex magicians at this point power their sigils with sexual energy and/or sexual fluids as these contain the very condensed essence of your power; and of course is one of the most entertaining ways of raising the necessary energy to power your spell, with or without a partner!

With the image of your sigil in mind, begin to make love with your partner. As you near the point of orgasm, try to hold back without quite crossing over, to build up a cone of energy between you both. The longer you can do this the more power you will raise. At the point of orgasm, visualize the energy from you both transferring into the sigil on the altar.

With you and your partner sated, and your sigil powered up, burn the sigil in your altar candle to activate it and send your spell out into the universe.

Sexy
Sigils

The Ancient Art: Traditional Sexual Remedies

Chapter 3

W e know from Church scholars and writers, both classical and medieval, that men and women have used herbs to heal and to control their fertility and childbearing since the earliest times. Often in conjunction with herbal medicine, they would call on the goddesses and gods to aid them in creating life (or to avoid conception) or as protectors during childbirth. Sexual magic, however, went way beyond the usual love potions or impotence spells performed on your neighbours' animals (as revenge, for instance, for some wrong the neighbours might have committed). Witchcraft and herb craft remained the primary female recourse to power over their own bodies, whether it was the power to attract love, to enjoy sex, to avoid unwanted sex, to conceive or not to conceive.

Sculptural evidence shows that special reverence was felt for women's sexual power. Sheela-na-gigs, for example, found mainly in Ireland but also in Britain, are carved figures of naked women – exuberant, vital Mother goddess figures displaying exaggerated vulvas. These descend from a very ancient veneration of the erotic, whose power is interpreted as blessing and protective. Rough-hewn and forceful, these stone figures cannot be interpreted as representing women as decorative or as submissive sexual objects.

For anyone interested in sex magic, it is fascinating to look at some of the traditional herbs and remedies that have been used for sex-related purposes in centuries past, as it will help to inform your modern-day practice.

Contraception

From time immemorial women have used various herbs and herbal compounds to prevent conception. We know that the ancient Egyptians used acacia gum (which contains compounds still used in spermicidal jellies). The Libyans made a drink from silphium (also known as silphion or laser), which is thought to have been a kind of giant fennel. It formed the mainstay of trade from the ancient city of Cyrene in Libya and was so much in demand internationally that it had become extinct by about 400 CE. The resin was extracted and used as a seasoning in cooking and as a remedy for all manner of ills – sore throat and coughs, fevers, indigestion, aches and pains, warts and all – and it was also highly prized as a contraceptive. It may be that, like some plants in the Apiaceae family (which includes various parsleys), notably the wild carrot, it had oestrogenic properties and

worked as an abortifacient, preventing or terminating pregnancies. Other abortifacient herbs mentioned by ancient Mediterranean writers were probably among those that women used in early medieval Europe: pennyroyal, artemisia, willow and rue. These were all herbs known to witches of the time, some with rich folkloric traditions. But while silphium seems to have been comparatively safe, these herbs can be actively dangerous to women – even harmless-sounding ones like nutmeg, in the form and quantities necessary to end or stop a pregnancy. They can have unpleasant or painful side-effects, or worse. Other early writers recommended mixtures that are quite clearly potentially fatal – like belladonna and honeysuckle.

In Asia, the bael fruit has a lot of uses – the fruit is eaten, sweets and a drink are made from it, and so is a detergent for washing clothes! The plant is used for medical purposes too – its astringent properties are useful in treating such ailments as dysentery. However, in Nepal the tree plays an important part in a fertility ritual for girls...although the leaves are said to cause abortion and sterility in women and it is therefore used as a contraceptive or abortifacient.

More recent German folk contraceptives include teas of marjoram, thyme, parsley and lavender (which can also abort), the root of worm fern and brake, known as 'prostitute root'. These too, though, can be harmful and should be avoided.

Northern sources refer to women using vaginal suppositories with cedar oil, or cabbage leaves, or fresh mandrake and other leaves – which may not sound wonderful but are an improvement on crocodile dung, one of the unpleasant ingredients favoured by the ancient Egyptians as contraceptives.

Another Ancient Egyptian Contraceptive

This was prescribed to prevent a woman from becoming pregnant for one, two or three years. First, a measure of acacia dates were ground finely and mixed with some honey. Then some seed-wool (like cotton wool) was soaked in the mixture and inserted into the vagina.

Fertility

Herbs and folk remedies have been used since ancient times to boost fertility as well as suppress it. The Javanese and Sumatran spice cubeb, or 'tailed pepper', is one such example. Prized as a cure for infertility and an aphrodisiac since at least the ninth century, it came to Europe via India through trade with the Arabs but was also widely used in Chinese medicine. In India, Unani physicians would use a paste of cubeb berries externally on the male and female genitals to intensify sexual pleasure. Arab physicians used it to cure infertility in their alchemical practices: in *The Book of One Thousand and One Nights*, a 'seed-thickening' mixture made with cubeb is given to Shams-al-Din, a wealthy childless merchant, with the instruction that he must eat it two hours before having sex with his wife. Nine months later, their child was born...

European pagans also have a long tradition of herbal remedies to draw on, some of which were ingested, or placed under a pillow or a mattress. Red clover blossom is one commonly cited example, often combined with peppermint in a brew. It's believed to be both a fertility booster and also a sexual stimulant. Other herbs that were thought to encourage pregnancy include nettle leaves, raspberry leaves (raspberry tea is still frequently recommended for pregnant women today as it is believed to tone the uterus), dong quai root, false unicorn root and primrose.

Trees, too, were believed to aid fertility. Mistletoe – also known as Witches' Broom – has a long association with witchcraft, its wood, leaves and berries used as charms to protect the wearer from harm. It was a sacred herb to the Druids, and in Norse mythology the herb was dedicated to the goddess of love, Freya. Carrying the berries was said to help a woman conceive (though please do not ingest mistletoe in any way as it is poisonous). Another tree, pine, also has pagan associations with fertility, as well as protection and prosperity. Pine branches would be used as brooms to banish negative energy, and are used in pagan handfasting (wedding) ceremonies today as a symbol of fertility. Pine cones can be carried as a fertility charm in the same way as mistletoe berries.

Dragon's Blood

This is the resin from the Dragon Tree, of which several species are native to south-east Asia and parts of Africa and South America. Add a pinch of the resin to love incenses to increase their potency and effectiveness. Or you can put some in sachets, or under the mattress to help cure impotency.

Of course, assuming that both partners want a child and have no reason to believe they are infertile, the first option if you want to conceive is to follow the natural cycle. It's quite logical that the day of ovulation is also an extremely powerful day for the woman, even apart from the fact that she can get pregnant then. It is her personal full moon, so if you wish to conceive you can make this a special occasion with a lovingly and carefully prepared sex magic ritual such as the one below.

FERTILITY SPELL
TO WELCOME
A NEW LIFE

৵৽

When you want to become pregnant and would like to give your child the best magical start in life, use this spell to evoke the aid of the gods to help you conceive.

You will need:

❖ *A few sunflower seeds*
❖ *Flour*
❖ *Water*
❖ *A small plant pot full of earth*

Method: Gather the items you need. Mix together half a cup of flour with some water to form a thick, but not solid, paste and set aside. Put a few of the sunflower seeds in a small bowl and place on your altar, along with the flowerpot full of earth.

Begin chanting 'Asase Yaa, Asase Yaa, Asase Yaa' (the name of the African earth goddess who is responsible for fertility), beginning quite softly as you will be chanting for a while, but gradually increasing in rhythm and volume.

Still chanting, form small egg-like balls of flour around each seed before planting them into the earth. When you have finished planting your eggs into the earth and your chanting has reached a crescendo, stop and say this prayer:

Asase Yaa!
Woman of the Earth,
Womb of the Earth,
As I plant these seeds in you
Help me grow and birth
New life

Child I welcome you
Asase Yaa!
Woman of the Earth
Womb of the Earth

After you have finished, place the pot in a sunny position, water and leave to sprout and grow!

The Woman and her Moon

On the days before menstruation a larger quantity of hormones circulates in the female body, not only increasing her emotions but also her magical power. During menstruation this extra power leaves her body. For that reason, menstruation is the most potent time for women magically, and the power of the menstrual blood along with other sexual secretions can be used in many ways. Blood has always been seen as one of the most potent seals on a vow to many cultures, but used magically it also has many other uses. It can anoint and consecrate your magical tools, or charge candles, cords and parchments, and a drop of blood on the finger could also be used to draw a symbol of power. In all cases, the blood carries the magician's life force essence, which is used to impart that energy elsewhere.

The use of menstrual blood in spells ensuring a husband's sexual fidelity is common in ancient and modern 'women's' folk magic, including Italian stregheria, Mexican brujeria, and African-American hoodoo. One way you can incorporate this practice yourself is to dab a little menstrual blood onto an amulet or talisman, which you can then give to your partner to ensure he or she will not stray! Of course, a less controversial way of ensuring a partner's fidelity is simply to work on maintaining the sexual spark and strength between you. And what better method of achieving this than to use an aphrodisiac…?

Aphrodisiacs

Aphrodite, Greek Goddess of Love, had a festival of her own, the Aphrodisiac, which was celebrated all over Greece but particularly in Athens and Corinth. It gave its name to denote anything – food, drink, potions – that acts on the mind to arouse sexual desire.

Historically, aphrodisiacs were sought to ensure fertility in times when both libido and potency could have been reduced by under-nourishment. Substances that represent seed or semen such as bulbs, eggs or snails were considered to have inherent sexual powers, while other foods became feted due to their resemblance to genitalia. Mythology provided another potent source for information about aphrodisiac ingredients. Aphrodite, the love goddess, was said to consider sparrows sacred because of their 'amorous nature', and for that reason they were included in various aphrodisiac brews – not exactly a thought that would get most of us going these days.

There was not always agreement upon which foods were actually aphrodisiacs but the list of traditional candidates included anise, basil, carrot, salvia, gladiolus root, orchid bulbs, pistachio nuts, rocket (arugula), sage, sea fennel, turnips, skink flesh (a type of lizard) and river snails.

In ancient Egypt, lettuce was thought to be the favourite food of the fertility god, Min. He was depicted as a god with an erect penis, wearing a feathered crown and carrying a flail. A species of lettuce called cos was his sacred plant, as it grows tall and upright and secretes a milky substance when pressed. Very sexy – and believed by the ancient Egyptians to have aphrodisiac qualities. They also considered fennel, ginger, pomegranates, coriander in wine, or radishes mixed with honey to have aphrodisiac qualities, too. Some of the more unusual aphrodisiacs included pearls dissolved in a cup of wine and baboon faeces. And as for onions, priests who had vowed celibacy were forbidden to eat them in case they got carried away and desecrated themselves!

Here are a few of the traditional herbal remedies believed to be effective nowadays – though please be aware that any substances ingested might cause side-effects, particularly if taken alongside other drugs, so please consult your doctor if you are unsure:

Maca

This hardy plant has been cultivated in the Andes for thousands of years, both for food and for its medicinal properties. Related to the turnip and radish, it is grown as a root vegetable. It is highly nutritious and prized as an adaptogen – a natural product that increases the body's resistance to stress and fatigue – and as an aphrodisiac. It provides sustained physical energy and immunostimulation, and many claim it is nature's answer to Viagra. Maca is rich in essential minerals such as selenium, calcium, magnesium and iron, amino acids, sterols and alkaloids. Like most adaptogens, the effects are most prominent with regular use, and one or two teaspoons of the powdered dried root a day is the usual intake, though it can be found in capsule form.

Muira Puama

Sometimes called 'potency wood', this is among the most valued herbs from the Amazon, and is believed to be a powerful aphrodisiac. Other outstanding benefits include increased energy and stamina, mental clarity, balanced hormones, and reduced symptoms associated with male and female impotence, erectile dysfunction, menstruation and the menopause.

All parts of muira puama have been used medicinally, but the bark and roots are the most-utilized parts of the plant. Since many of the plant's most active constituents are not water-soluble it is best to prepare this plant as a tincture (dissolved in alcohol) and take 2-4 ml of a 4:1 tincture twice daily. Boiling the tincture for 20 minutes will help to extract the non-water-soluble essential oils, terpenes, gums and resins found in the bark and root which have been linked to muira puama's beneficial effects. (Traditionally, it was soaked in rum and buried for a week.) It also makes a delicious and potent tea.

Suma

Amazonian tribes have made use of Suma Root Powder as a sexual tonic and energy booster for at least 300 years. It is believed to improve sexual performance, and is also used to ease the symptoms of chronic fatigue. It contains anabolic-like substances and concentrations of amino acids, vitamins and trace minerals.

Yohimbe Bark Powder

The Yohimbe tree grows throughout the African nations of Cameroon, Gabon and Zaire, and for centuries the bark has been used as a sexual stimulant. Indeed an extract from the tree, yohimbine hydrochloride, is often used today under medical supervision to treat erectile dysfunction.

WARNING: Yohimbe is also a short-term MAO inhibitor and should be used with caution, especially if you have high blood pressure. Yohimbe should not be taken with any food or drink containing tyramines (cheese, chocolate, beer, aged meats, nuts, etc.). Also, do not use with anti-depressants, sedatives, antihistamines, caffeine or amphetamines.

Satisfy
the
Senses

Chapter 4

here are no instant recipes for success with sex, but there are ways we can be sure that the scene is set when attending to our sexual desires. Our desires are all rooted in the senses, so it is the obvious place to start on the journey to sexual bliss.

Sight

This is the sense that is most relied upon in the modern world; the phrase 'love at first sight' shows us how, consciously or unconsciously, this is the sense we use first in the hunt for a mate. Indeed, visual representations of sex have always been a source of titillation and discussion, from graffitti in Roman times right up to the internet today; it seems as soon as some new technology is developed the lustful side of humanity is never far behind.

Why not arrange a love-in with your paramour, watch erotic films, and practise your sensuous spell casting? Do the films give you any ideas for play-acting? Dress as one of the characters, cast a glamour and feel the power change. *Have fun!*

Remember too that presentation is the first ingredient in this cocktail of the senses, so be confident that you have done everything you can to be looking your best: put on your favourite outfit, comb your hair, brush your teeth and don't forget to make sure your underwear is clean! After all, if you spend an afternoon at the salon, then bathe, prepare yourself and enact your spell, nothing will shatter the moment faster than the sight of your ten-year-old 'lucky' pulling pants – however strong the magic.

The image you present to the world, like your confidence, is a reflection of the divine within each of us; this inner confidence can be woven into a spell known as a 'glamour'. One of the most renowned cases in Celtic legend is when King Arthur's father, Uther Pendragon, asked Merlin to cast a glamour over him so that he appeared to the chaste Ygrainee as her returning husband. He was so successful that she welcomed him with open arms and nine months later gave birth to Arthur...

As we don't have the luxury of having Merlin on hand to do our bidding we have to rely on our own talents and imaginations to cast this type of spell.

CASTING A GLAMOUR

ॐ

You will need:

❖ Rose or amaranth petals
❖ Vanilla candles/Incense/Oil
❖ A favourite picture of yourself or a picture of someone you think has those glamorous qualities you'd like

Method: Create your sacred space in the bathroom and light the candles, incense or oil burner while the bath fills.

When it is ready for you, scatter the flower petals in it.

As you lie in the water, slow your breathing and relax into a meditative state. Think about how you felt as you were when the picture was taken and how you want to be – relaxed, happy, confident, in control, beautiful. As the warmth of the water soaks into your body, imagine these feelings filling your body once more, expelling the old you.

Concentrate on the image you would like to project and say these words:

> *Earth, Air, Fire and Water*
> *Let the Goddess's beauty*
> *Shine through me.*

*Casting
a Glamour*

Keep repeating this mantra until the bath cools, then rise from your bath like a newborn Venus from the waves. Staying 'in character', prepare yourself for the evening of adventure, as the walking embodiment of the Goddess. Do remember that you don't have to restrict yourself to the ancient pantheons: the twentieth century has seen some of the most desirable goddesses of its own, in the worlds of film, television and music. To keep the glamour going will take practice but once you regularly start to invite those goddess qualities in, you will begin to find it easier to let her stay.

MORNING DEW
SPELL

❧❧

The dew in May has always been the witch's beauty secret. An old proverb associated with the May festival of Beltane says that you will retain your beauty longer if you wash your face in the first dew of May. This spell, however, can be done during a waxing (growing) moon in any month, and will be nearly as effective. For this you will need:

❖ *One wide bowl*
❖ *Vanilla oil*

Method: On a Thursday evening during a waxing moon, meditate quietly at your altar to achieve the tranquil state needed to prepare yourself for this spell, before taking your bowl outdoors and placing it on the grass. Anoint the rim with a few drops of vanilla oil, gaze at the moon and, thinking of the serene and beautiful goddess Venus, make a statement of your desire to enhance your looks.

On Friday morning – Venus's day, the planet ruling personal appearance – use your hands to bathe your face in the collected dew. Bathe other visible parts of your body with any remaining water. Be sure to visualize clearly the outcome you desire as often as you can from the time you first touch the bowl until the spell is done.

Morning Dew

GLAMOROUS BEAUTY SPELL

❧◦❧

This spell will make you look irresistable to all who lay eyes on you.

You will need:

❖ Rose petals
❖ Damiana
❖ Ginger
❖ Dong quai
❖ Coriander
❖ Primrose flowers
❖ Small green glass jar
❖ Ylang-ylang oil
❖ Pink candle
❖ Venus oil, rose oil or perfume
❖ Small mirror
❖ Rose water

Method: On a night of Venus (Friday), after some quiet time in meditation, mix some rose petals, damiana, ginger, dong quai, coriander, and primrose flowers and put into the green glass jar. Add sufficient boiling water to make a pot of tea large enough to contain seven small cups of tea, and place on your altar to steep and cool down.

Take a bath with a few drops of ylang-ylang oil and a handful of rose petals. When you've got out and dried yourself, go to your altar nude and light a pink candle anointed with Venus oil or rose oil or perfume. Place a small mirror on the altar, gaze into it deeply and say:

Soft, my skin as Diana's
Smouldering eyes as Venus,
Sensuous as Erzulie.
Figures of fire that shift and change,
Change me, now,
To a creature of beauty,
Blessed be the Goddess of Love.

Repeat each night for seven nights,
drinking one cup of the cold tea per
night, leaving the remaining tea on the
altar until the spell is finished. Wash
your face with rose water upon waking
each morning.

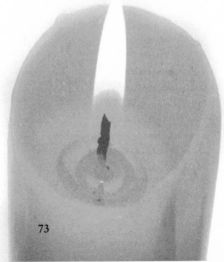

MOULIN ROUGE
SPELL

❧❧

This is for when you need to make a big entrance!

You will need:

❖ *4 red candles*
❖ *Cinnamon spice or oil*

Method: For this spell wear colourful clothes, flamboyant and luscious. If you really cannot bear to venture out in anything but black make sure you wear opulent jewellery –

stones of topaz, sapphire and ruby.

Anoint four red candles with cinnamon spice or oil. Light the candles and place them around you, so you stand in the centre of them. You need to invoke the blessings of the night when glamour and mystery abound. Recite the following words:

All Hail, Hecate! Guardian of the night
Mistress of deep mysteries
Bless me so that I radiate a beautiful light
And bewitch all held in my sight.

In your mind's eye see the flames leap up and join above your head, spiralling into the cosmos. Know that you are the centre of all beauty and glamour in the universe.

Centre of all Beauty

Scent

Scent has the power to trigger long-forgotten memories, instantly returning us to another time, or to invoke a mood in an instant. We use this phenomenon to sweeten the air as well as to help us to achieve our meditative 'otherly' state when we connect with the divine, celebrate the mysteries and perform our magic. Scents also act as a medium to send and carry our prayers, desires and spells out into the aether. We can use fragrance by burning scented candles, incense or oil floating on water in a burner to indicate whether we wish to make offerings to a certain deity or to mark an occasion such as one of the eight sabbatical festivals. It all helps to create the sense that we are doing something sacred away from the humdrum of our everyday lives.

Incense and Oil Burning

'Each waft of smoke contains the energy of the earth, the sun, the rain, the wind, the stars, the moon and the sky.' – Peacock Angel.

There are two main types of incense: combustible, which contains additives to help it burn and comes in the form of cones, sticks or other shapes, and non-combustible, which is usually loose and must be sprinkled into a fire or over smouldering embers to release its properties. For ease and convenience most witches use stick incense, but given the choice will readily make their own mixtures, which gives more range and subtlety to the power of the incense.

If you can make a herbal blend for a tea, you can make an incense. The loose varieties are the easiest to start with. As you mix your blend you can charge it with your intent, gaining another magical layer to your spell-casting. The basic materials can be drawn together from a base of resins, gums and oils, with leaves, barks, flowers, roots and wood forming the rest. Some blends will have the most magical properties – but be warned, they might not smell so sweet! Experiment with individual materials and get to know your ingredients before you go ahead and make vast batches of incense.

Burning your incense is easy if you use the self-igniting charcoal discs sold in most pagan, occult and craft shops: holding the disc with tongs, light one edge until the saltpetre has ignited all the way across the disc, then place it in your censer. This can be any sort of container from a saucer with salt or sand to disperse the heat, all the way up to elaborate vessels hung on chains as used by churches. Once the charcoal disc is an even, deep, cherry red with greying edges it is ready; start by dropping small pinches of incense onto the disc then lean back and note how the ingredient burns. Note how the initial sweet smell can change or turn bitter after a time; some, like fine wines, have a long aftertaste, others fade quickly; the most important thing is to be able to tune in to the vibrations and character of each material.

To make your blend, it is easy to consult a recipe book and follow that recipe but once you have done your research do not be afraid to experiment with other ingredients, making sure that the corresponding properties match those you require for your blend and that you have consulted a good herbalist with up-to-date advice. Here are a few of the most sensual blends to try.

SENSUAL LOVING INCENSE

Burn this when spell casting to boost sensuality.

- ❖ 1 part cinnamon bark
- ❖ 1 part cedar bark
- ❖ a few drops of rose oil

GODDESS BLEND

❧❧

For use when evoking a female deity.

- ❖ 2 parts benzoin (a balsamic resin)
- ❖ 1 part rosebuds
- ❖ a few drops patchouli oil
- ❖ a few drops rose oil

GOD BLEND

❧❧

For use when evoking a male deity.

- ❖ 3 parts frankincense
- ❖ 2 parts myrrh
- ❖ 1/2 part bay leaves
- ❖ 1/2 part dried orange rind
- ❖ a few drops olive oil

Boost Sensuality

Pheromones

A pheromone is a chemical signal, usually detected by the sense of smell, which is produced by a living organism to transmit a message to other creatures (some even argue that this ancient form of communication works between vegetal and animal species). There are alarm pheromones (how often have you heard the phrase 'They can smell fear'?), food trail pheromones (ants for instance will 'call' other ants to a source of food), territorial pheromones (many mammals will urinate to mark their territory), sex pheromones, and many others. In mammals and reptiles, pheromones may be detected by Jacobson's organ, which lies between the nose and mouth, although most are detected by regular nasal membranes. Sex pheromones are nature's own 'come hither' spells, and indicate the need for sex and breeding. Certain butterflies can detect a potential mate from as many as ten kilometres away!

Pheromones are even thought by some to be responsible for the way in which women who live or work together over a length of time will synchronize their menstrual cycles. Or indeed could also be why two people can be attracted to each other for no obvious reason when meeting for the first time, or, similarly, why two people might take an instant but irrational dislike to each other. The most common claims for pheromones though are internet advertisements proclaiming that products containing artificially extracted sexual pheromones can act as an aphrodisiac, though I would never endorse buying these – why pay for something artificial when Mother

Nature has provided us with the real thing?

The body starts to produce pheromones after reaching puberty, which could explain why it is from that age that most people begin to feel attracted to others. Pheromones are given off from the body in sweat from two different types of gland: those distributed all over the body, which in general regulate temperature, and those glands located in the armpits and genital regions, which are the ones that give off the secret messages to potential sexual partners,

especially when hot and aroused. That is why most pagans prefer their partners clean and groomed but not smothered in strong and potentially damaging artificially scented products, which could potentially block out the subtle and sensual scent of our own natural bodies.

Sound

Music

Music in all its forms has the power to trigger all kinds of emotional response and memories, much as smells do. Magically, we can use this to add another layer in either the preparation or enactment of a spell; either to achieve the trance state or create a sonic mood for the spell.

As every ancient shaman and modern DJ knows, there are different tunes for different parts of the event, and some instinctively or deliberately touch on the magical side of music by using instruments ascribed to a different element for each set of beats, to build up energy, excitement and intensity. Drumming has long been the way to induce and lead a magical dance and trance.

Earthy instruments include the heart-like pounding and pulsing instruments such as the xylophone, rattle and drums; bells, gongs, sistrum and cymbals quiver like water; flutes, pipes and all wind instruments hum through the air; and all plucked, dancing stringed instruments display their fiery nature (just think of the flamenco!).

For those of us lucky enough to be able to play these instruments competently, the ritual can be led by the music. However, even if you don't play arranged music, a regular beat on a drum or a chiming bell or Tibetan singing bowl can be regularly used to 'drum up' and invoke a female deity, with pipes and guitars used to call to a male deity and to clear ritual spaces.

Singing, a combination of speech and music, is another highly effective way to raise the energy needed for magic. Whether a Wiccan song or a Buddhist chant, the exact words are not important: it is the vibrations within the body and the opening of the heart and throat chakras that literally 'give voice' to your will and desires.

Poetry/Prose

Could there be anyone who does not thrill to the sound of their lover's voice? And who could resist the subtle sensuality of having their partner read them a sonnet or love poem? Try this sympathetic magic spell to bewitch your lover using just the sound of your voice.

POPPET POEM

SPELL

ঌ৽৽৶

You will need:

❖ *A small poppet*
❖ *A love poem – either one
you have written yourself,
or one you have found
in an anthology*

Method: Make your poppet – a small figure no bigger than your hand fashioned out of cloth scraps, wax, clay, papier mâché or similar. It doesn't have to be recognizable as your beloved, only to be clearly a human figure. Alternatively, you could use a soft toy or figure that is significant to you both.

If you have a lock of your lover's hair attach this to the poppet to strengthen the link between it and your sweetheart, all the while visualizing that this is your beloved. Draw both ears and heart onto the figure, then place the doll on the altar.

Recite your poem to the doll as though you were seducing your lover, thinking about all the amorous adventures you will have. Repeat until you are happy that the message has been heard and felt by the universe.

When you next meet, softly speak some of the words you used and watch as your beloved is drawn to you, heart aflame.

Seduce your Lover

Phone Sex

A spell is a way of expressing your desires and needs and sending them into the aether, so the mobile phone can be the perfect tool for the spell-caster on the move. Of course you can call your sweetheart and whisper sweet nothings and naughtinesses to him or her direct, but what can you do if there is neither the time nor the place for talk or text conversations?

Try this quick spell to let your will be known.

CALL TO THE AETHER

❧

You will need:

❖ *A mobile phone*

Method: Type in your message of desire to the one you want, then dedicate the message to Ganesha as

opener of the ways, remover of
obstacles. Mercury is also good for
this type of spell in his role as god of
communication.

Next spell out the name of your
sweetheart on the number pad, taking
care not to make a real number, then
send and your spell is complete.

You may get a network 'message
undeliverable' back, but you will know
that the message has got through to the
right channels when you next meet up!

Magical Music

Make a sexy selection of your
favourite songs, the ones that
express the way you feel, and put
the playlist on a CD, MP3 player
or an iPod for your lover. As the
music plays, each revolution of
the disc or drive expresses your
carnal desires.

Touch

With massage oils you get to satisfy the
sense of touch as well as smell,
with the oil gliding silkily on the skin
and the dreamy aromas providing a
heady combination. Choose a good-
quality oil imbued with vanilla, ylang-
ylang or your lover's favourite scent,
consecrate it to one of your favourite
deities, and then treat your beloved to
a full body massage.

The intensity of your massage can
progress to intense stimulation by using
different sensations on your lover's
body; fire (candle wax, dropped from
at least 30 cm) and ice (cubes), or fur
and feathers (gently stroked). This is
further increased when your partner is
blindfolded or gently restrained so that
he or she has no choice other than
to concentrate on the sensations you
are providing.

Change places with your lover or
simply dispense with the foreplay and
make love until the point of climax,

when you can release all that high-voltage energy into whatever spell you desire.

A lovely variation of a sigil spell is to paint the final form onto your lover as the sex begins, so the sigil is charged and then activated at the same time – especially if you paint the sigil with something edible such as chocolate!

Which leads us to the kingdom of taste…

Taste

It could be argued that the ability to combine base ingredients into complex and mouth-watering dishes is an art in itself, but when you consider the properties of the plants and herbs we use in these meals it becomes clear that many of us have been practising basic kitchen witchery without even realizing it! Whereas people who are not attuned to a magical life will think the food tastes just fine, those of us who can appreciate the subtle application of a little magic in the kitchen will reap the reward in the bedroom too. A list of common herbs and their corresponding properties is provided at the back of the book.

Different foods and drinks have always been served to reflect the different festivals of the year; special harvest loaves at Lammas, hot cross buns at the spring equinox, summer fruit pudding at Litha or chestnut soup at Yule.

There are also plenty of ingredients thought to be the foods of lovers, having various aphrodisiac properties claimed for them. But beware! By all means try these foods if you want, but remember that different cultures, in different times, find aphrodisiac qualities in all manner of foods; remember too that the quest for the ultimate aphrodisiac may also be rather heavy on the pocket. As the food and drink we consume becomes part of us, blends with us and stays with us, aphrodisiacs are really a matter of personal taste and adventure.

Sharing a favourite dinner at home with a loved one, when the whole evening has been prepared with magic and affection, is far more effective than focusing on the individual ingredients. Plus, of course, you don't have to worry about paying the bill before you retire to your boudoir!

As you develop your magical repertoire you will see that magic is a part of daily life so don't neglect your first five senses in the search for the sixth.

Sacred Sexuality: Contacting the God/Goddess within

Chapter 5

You are a goddess!
You are a god!

How many of us remember this in our day-to-day lives? How many of us invoke the energy of the divine prior to coming together to celebrate our sexual selves? How often do we give the gods an opportunity to experience pleasure embodied, to make love, to do what they are meant to do? Sex is an important part of the cycle of life for us as humans and for the planet as a whole. Sacred sex is a way to connect the self with the divine, to tap into the power of the divine, and is easily one of the most enjoyable methods of raising energy to power a spell!

'To know the Divine is to be Divine'

The aim here is to try to touch the divine by bringing the qualities and attributes of the gods into our lives and into our magic. The power of sex has been harnessed as long as there have been people, but over time this communion became formalized and elaborate rituals and traditions arose with the result that often only the ritual is remembered and the reason forgotten (for example the ancient custom of throwing confetti at a wedding was originally a pagan fertility rite, as they would shower the couple with grain to ensure a fruitful union). When there are so many consumer products and services clamouring for our attention in the name of the 'goddess within', is it any wonder that pagans today are also searching to reclaim something of the actual power and grace of the Goddess? Who can say that there is not a bit of Hera the homemaker, Aphrodite the love maker, Pan the partygoer, Persephone the mystic, Ares the warlike leader or Artemis the nature lover and defender in all of us? Whether we see the goddesses and gods from a religious point of view or as archetypes, it pays to get to know them before inviting them in to help you with your magic.

There are many forms of sacred sex, from many religions and traditions, most of which date from the times when attitudes towards religion were a lot more sex-positive, and sexual practice was not only more celebratory but more magically charged. Eastern Tantric, Taoist and Yoga traditions, Graeco-Roman love cults, Egyptian and Babylonian priestesses, travelling performers and dancers have all been the caretakers of these ancient secrets that with a little help we can rediscover today.

'Who knows God, becomes God.' – Mundaka Upanishad

Hieros Gamos and Other Sacred Sex Rites

In the earliest cultures, the feminine was all-powerful and life-creating; all over the world, statues, temples and shrines are found with figures of a Mother Earth goddess, heavy-set, bountiful, curvy and sexual.

Some 5,500 years ago, the ancient Sumerians, who glorified eroticism and sexual intercourse, would inaugurate their king in a ritual ceremony called by the Greeks *Hieros Gamos*, or 'Sacred Marriage'. To the Sumerians the Goddess, as the giver of life and fertility, was the divine power who gave the right to rule, and the would-be king would have to prove himself to her sexually. The priestess or *hierodule*, acting as the earthly embodiment of the Goddess Inanna (Sumer's Venus or Aphrodite) would have sex with the ruler of the country in front of the temple-goers, who would watch the entire ritual, offering encouragement and shouting their wild approval at its successful completion.

Centuries later, the Greek historian Herodotus (484-425 BC), observed in Babylon a similar view of sex as a sacred ritual, writing:

'Babylonian custom compels every woman of the land once in her life to sit in the temple of love and have intercourse with some stranger. The men pass and make their choice. It matters not what be the sum of money; the woman will never refuse, for that were a sin, the money being by this act made sacred. After their intercourse she has made herself holy in the sight of the goddess and goes away to her home.'

This practice came to be seen in later times as prostitution, in societies that were less sex positive and which valued the Goddess considerably less. Quintus Curtius, the historian who accompanied Alexander the Great on his conquests, wrote, round about 325 BC, 'There is none other more corrupt than this people…Fathers and mothers suffered their daughters to prostitute themselves to their guests for silver and husbands were not less indulgent with respect to their wives.'

In ancient Egypt, as in Sumeria, sex was joyfully celebrated. Egyptian sacred 'prostitutes' were probably highly regarded within Egyptian society because of their association with different gods and goddesses, such as Bes and Hathor. There is no evidence that these women were paid for these fertility-related acts, so the word 'prostitute' is probably an incorrect term. Although a woman would be severely punished for committing adultery once she was married, unmarried women could indulge in unrestricted sexual activity. One theory is that this was a part of a 'coming-of-age' ritual, with a practical aspect: fertility was of paramount importance to the ancient Egyptians and here was a way to test a woman's fecundity. And as motherhood was venerated, and gave a woman a much higher status in society, pregnancy was something to be proud of in ancient Egypt.

A similar practice was also found in southern Asia (and survives today in various forms). The Hindu *devadasi*, like the geisha of Japan, are a much maligned and misunderstood group who have been persistently excluded and repressed for many years. They were originally a varied caste of temple servants who were dedicated or 'married' to the temple's God, and who undertook a wide range of different activities within the temple. They were dancers, singers, actresses and even political advisers, and many also integrated sexual practices into their vocations. Their skills and talents meant that, unlike most women in southern Asia, they could live independently of men and often enjoyed considerable wealth and influence. As with the accomplished geisha, most *devadasi* only ever had one patron.

More recently, a few neopagan groups have actually revived a kind of *Hieros Gamos* in a fertility rite where public sexual conjunction symbolizing the planting of a seed into Mother Earth takes place at a Beltane ceremony, but it is something not everyone would feel comfortable practising. These days sex is not generally seen as an essential religious experience, as ennobling and uplifting, as something which could take you closer to the gods rather than alienate you from them. Perhaps it is time to remind contemporary society how to bring the natural power of the divine into our lives, through adding a little magic to our sex lives.

Connecting with Kama

Kama is a Hindu god of love, who brings fire and passion to your being. His song is represented by the fifth note of Krishna's flute as the Kama Gayatri mantra, the sound of divine passion, the sound that stole the hearts of Radha and other women, making them forget everything and run to the forest to meet their divine lover.

Chant the Kama Gayatri mantra to attract the perfect lover or to revive the romantic spirit between you and your existing partner. Chant to become sexually attractive to others, to have magnetic eyes and lips made for kisses; this practice is also a great aid in perking up your own desire. If your love life gets stale, the Kama Gayatri mantra will turn things around, releasing an avalanche of sensuality that was hiding inside of you. Working with Kama develops the sexual side of you, making you a sensual, joyful and desirable lover. Offer Kama love by dedicating your most playful, noisy lovemaking to him.

KAMA MANTRA

❧❦

This is a classic love spell with its roots going back to ancient Sanskrit tales about Kama in the *Kama Sutra*.

You will need:

* ❖ A picture of the god Kama
* ❖ A red candle
* ❖ Small bowls or saucers
* ❖ Honey
* ❖ Rose petals
* ❖ A picture of your loved one (optional)

92

Method: In front of the picture of Kama burn the red candle, and in the small bowls or saucers offer honey and fragrant red and pink rose petals. Feel the delight of love enter your body and entire being. Smell the roses and chant the Kama Gayatri mantra to become sweet and desirable like honey. You can also put a picture of the one you desire or the picture of your present lover on the altar to fall in love with him/her again/even more. See the love god in your lover, as you recite the prayer. Celebrate love in any way you imagine as the spirit of Kama fills you…

Aum Kamadevaye Vidmahe,
Pushp' Vanaye Dhi-Mahi
Tanno Kamah Prachdayat

Translation:
Let us contemplate Kama,
The God of Love,
Let this power direct us.

A Classic Love Spell

Erotic Dancing

As well as being great fun, dance has been used in ritual practice since ancient times. It's also a magical act, for physical movement releases energy from the body, the same energy used in magic. This 'secret' was discovered early, and so dance was incorporated into magic and ritual to raise energy, to alter consciousness or simply to honour the Goddess and God with ritual performances.

Group dances, such as the spiral dance, are often performed in modern coven workings. In individual workings, however, you're bound by no tradition or choreographed steps. Feel free to move in any manner you wish, no matter how child-like or 'savage' it may seem. When practising magic, many Wiccans perform a short spell or ritual manipulations of some kind and then perform the real magic: raising and channelling magical energy. They often move in a increasingly faster clockwise circle around the altar, either alone or with a coven, watching the candles flaming on the altar, smelling the incense, overwhelming themselves with chanting and intense visualization.

When the practitioner has reached the point of no return, the exact moment when the body can raise and channel no more energy, the power is released toward the magical goal. To do this, some Wiccans collapse to the ground, signalling the end of 'The Dance'. Dancing is also used to attune to the deities of nature as well as to raise energy. Dance as the wild wind; as the stream rushing down a mountain; as a flame flickering from a lightning-struck tree; as grains of sand bouncing off each other in a gale; as flowers unfolding their brilliance on a sunny summer afternoon.

As you dance, using whatever movements you wish, open yourself to the gods and goddesses.

Think for a moment of the whirling dervishes, the untamed gypsy dances of Europe, the sensuous belly dancing of the Middle East, and the sacred hula of Hawaii. Dance the paths to deity.

Playtime: Using Sex to Create Magic

Chapter 6

*N*ow that you have learned a few of the basic magical techniques, it is time to expand your horizons and set off on your own exploration of sex magic...

There are many methods, but the sole purpose of sex magic is not, as many people imagine, to attract or get more sex. Neither does the definition apply solely to rituals such as the sacred marriage of the God and Goddess, the Great Rite, either actual or symbolic. Here, in this sense, sex magic is about raising energy through the use of sex or sexuality and focusing and utilizing the energy for a specific goal agreed in advance.

How Sex Magic Works

First of all you need to decide exactly what you want to achieve with your magic. You could be the most powerful of sorcerers, but without will or purpose all of your best magic and spell-work will remain as vague as smoke, and will waft around ineffectually until dissipated. Your goal could be something material such as attaining a new job or housing. It could also be something less tangible such as the healing of yourself, another person, Mother Earth...

Your intent might be the improvement of an existing relationship or the creation of a new one. You may wish to develop certain qualities in yourself, or to create an excellent artistic piece. You may wish to embrace the inner lover, and establish a stronger connection with your higher self. You may wish to charge an amulet, talisman, or magical tools, and so on... Whatever it might be, it should be something you wish for with all your heart – deeply desired wishes create the strongest magic.

Your goal established, then create something that makes it possible to concentrate with precision on your goal/intent during the ritual. This can be a short verbal affirmation, your personal mantra. During the ritual you can repeat the whole affirmation. An alternative is to reduce this affirmation to a single word that covers its central idea; this will be your magical word. For example, the affirmation 'I am a successful businessperson' becomes 'Success'; 'I request the universe to send me the best possible lover, or partner' becomes 'Lover' or 'Partner'. The idea behind it is that your subconscious now knows your full intent, so it is sufficient to repeat just your magical word during the ritual.

Alternatively, you can create a visualization of the desired reality. Start with intensely picturing the desired situation; feel your happiness about it, visualize it as bright and detailed as you can. If you do a working for somebody else, for instance a healing, envisage their joy and enthusiasm in the new situation. When your visualization is complete, tell your mind that this is your focus, then mentally store it in your subconscious. If you find it hard to do this without an external stimulus, you can do a drawing of what you want, or you can use a symbolic representation of your desire – an appropriate tarot card, rune, sigil, astrological or other symbol, for instance.

If you are conducting the ritual for someone else (do ask first) it can be helpful to have a photograph or an item belonging to that person.

You can, of course, use combinations of all of the above.

Once you have decided on your goal and method, you can then perform the ritual. There are two techniques, depending on whether you have chosen to use an affirmation/ mantra/Word of Power, or a visualization.

Affirmation/Mantra

If you have chosen to work with an affirmation, start by arousing yourself and/or your partner by any sexual

THE LOVERS.

activity you wish to use until you almost reach orgasm. Meanwhile keep on repeating your magical word or words; you can say it out loud or repeat it silently. When you are at the brink of orgasm back off by stopping all genital stimulation and all pelvic movements and relax the muscles in the pelvic floor. Breathe deeply and concentrate even more on your mantra. After a while, build up more excitement, backing off again just before the point of no return. This way you build up a great amount of sexual magical energy and deep erotic sensations; you may reach a state of sexual trance. After several times coming close, you wish to sweep all of your intent into the universe, let orgasm happen and – here comes the most important part – keep on affirming during orgasm, with full mental concentration, call out loud your magical word(s) and don't mind the neighbours! Take care: if you lose focus during orgasm, you will have had great sex but no magical ritual.

Continue the ritual until both (or all) partners have reached orgasm.

Visualization

If you prefer working with a visualization, place your image or symbolic representation (if using) by the bed where you can see it. Start making love with your partner or masturbating, no longer thinking about the visualization. At the brink of orgasm back off, recall or look at your visualization and breathe your orgasmic energy into it. Continue the rhythm of arousal and backing off several times. Just before orgasm recall the visualization from your mind and breathe/channel your orgasm into it.

If you are a woman capable of having multiple orgasms (a series of orgasms quickly after one another), just enjoy them during the ritual and end with the final orgasm. If you are a man, here's the good news – men can learn to have multiples too; by coming close then backing off just before the point of no return several times, men can experience all the feelings of an orgasm without having an ejaculation. Some men have a series of small orgasms, and some experience them as bigger orgasms. If you can do this, end the ritual with final orgasm/ejaculation. Not all men know that most women need clitoral stimulation to reach orgasm; although there are erotic areas in the vagina, most women need the pressure of their partner's pubic bone against the clitoris or stimulation by hand during intercourse to reach orgasm.

After orgasm you may wish to confirm your magic with the words 'So mote it be,' and to give thanks to the God and Goddess and your partner.

It is important to stay close the first minutes after intercourse, with your genitals close together (unless of course you are using a condom in order to avoid a sexually transmitted disease or pregnancy). There are two reasons for this:

★ When you have sex, your chakras open up and after orgasm you're completely open with part of your energy swirling around you. You need some time to let the energies realign. If one partner rushes away after orgasm you can feel very disappointed, lonely and exhausted for this reason.

★ After sex magic the sexual fluids of both men and women are charged with their magical intent; they can ethereally absorb this power for their wellbeing and health through the vaginal walls and the head of the penis. The charged sexual fluids can be used to power an amulet or talisman by smearing some on one; if the aim of your ritual was to gain money you can smear some on a coin or paper money and put it on your altar; or you can use the fluids to redraw the lines of a sigil. In sex magic the charged sexual fluids have become the sacred elixir of life, and

are in no way dirty (though it should
go without saying that if there's any
chance you or your partner might
have a sexually-transmitted disease,
you should avoid working with
sexual fluids). When you are doing
sex magic alone please know that
your sexual fluids form a complete
sacrament, although they now
contain only one polarity, not two –
in other words they do not benefit
from the magical energy which
results when male and female
polarities are joined together. That
said, the fact that a spell is performed
and combined with the practitioner's
will makes the sacrament complete.

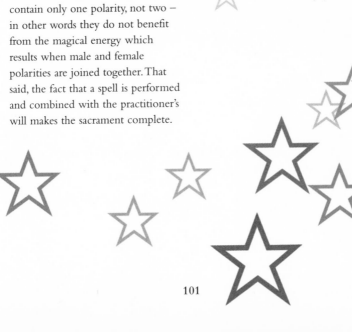

SPONTANEOUS
RITUALS

❧❧

Sometimes your hormones or energies are overflowing with the urgent need of a magical outlet but there is no time to prepare anything. If that's the case, try this virtual ritual.

Method: Start by visualizing your sacred workspace, wherever you are in reality. Next, open yourself to the universe, dedicating your energy to the flow, by reciting a mantra such as, 'I open up for my full human potential,' or the magical words, 'Open up.' If you're with a partner you can say, 'I honour your divinity,' or the magical word, 'Divinity.'

Enjoy the feeling of release and empowerment as you join yourself to the universe or deity. Reconfirm your mantra, then release your sacred space.

Honour your Divinity

Tantra

Sex magic is fairly well integrated into Eastern custom, with the Tao and Eastern thought maintaining that it is a desirable practice. There seems to be much less shame, guilt and repression in the East, in some ways, and energy and energy work is a commonly accepted idea – think about Chinese acupuncture. Then there is Tantra, an advanced form of spiritual communion and magical practice that is accessible to everyone, although the sex is just one part of the whole system. There are numerous books available, both text and erotic picture books, on the subject, and the average person can at least experiment in this area without having to undergo years of training in the mysteries of spiritual sexual practices.

In Western society, however, sex magic is seen as something shameful. The Christian fundamentalist principles are so engrained in our cultural attitudes, it's a wonder any of us get together at all. As pagans we can begin to overcome this attitude by revelling in every opportunity to celebrate our bodies and our sexuality and by worshipping the old gods, Nature and the Earth.

Safe Zones

As with any non-magical activity – YOU MUST PLAY SAFE! You are no longer working responsibly if you or your partner undertakes a ritual or spell only for it to be incomplete, spiral out of control or have the participants working against each other, unintentionally or otherwise. Would you take a new lover without taking precautions to protect you both? Of course not.

Choose and design your spell carefully so that all the basics are covered before you begin, being prepared to think on your feet to modify your spell to respond to any unplanned circumstances; it may not be safe to stop halfway through, for example. Unlike sexy role-playing games, safe words do not work here! Spells are most effective when the caster is relaxed, focused and assured, without nervousness or over-confidence.

So how do you create the safe zone? To work out the how and why of a spell most magicians spend huge amounts of time and energy using divinations, to find the who, what, where, why, when and how of a situation to see if an intervention or spell is indeed the best course of action. If the answers to these questions all point to some action, the how and when often become apparent.

Divination

Divination is, in essence, a way of taking a peek into the future, a way of asking the universe what might be. In psychological terms, divination can be seen as a method of searching within ourselves for the answers that are not immediately apparent, and using tools or props to allow these answers to externalize.

Another way to look at divination would be to say that it allows us to make contact with the otherworldly spirits, guides or gods, and ask for their guidance. If you have a favourite or patron deity they can often be the first port of call, but if you have a question which relates to a particular area of life it may well be best to also call upon an expert in that field and use the appropriate method.

There are many methods of divination, from ancient shamanic bone casting, rune reading, tea leaf reading, crystal ball gazing, tarot, mirror or water scrying, all the way up to TV scrying, cloud watching and online oracles. As with other areas of magic it pays to be familiar with the methods and forms but most practitioners find with practice which type of divination they are most competent and comfortable with.

Practising Sex Magic

A good example of a situation that needs careful consideration of the ethics and outcomes is when sex magic is utilized specifically to influence other people, as opposed to using it to alter a situation. There are more spells for love and sex than any other type of spell, covering everything from simply attracting a partner, right the way up the scale to targeting and permanently binding someone to you forever and a day. All very well, but let's just remember you don't want to attract *everyone* in the neighbourhood and, at the other extreme, binding *for ever* is an awfully long time. Who knows, you may not like each other much after the first century together…

Warnings aside, the main reason for making love or magic is to enjoy yourself, and having partners to do it with can double the fun! Some people are going to have an adverse response when it comes to anything sensual or

erotic. But much of the negative response seems to come from the fact that people think it has to do with deception or manipulation. It does not: sex magic just doesn't work if both partners are not focused and willing participants.

A magical-sexual partnership can be one of the most rewarding and pleasurable forms of bond, making coercive binding unnecessary and undesirable. This mutual binding can last for the length of the spell working, or indeed longer, as with most pagan 'hand-fastings', where the marriage or union is renewable after a year and a day. Other bondings can be decided in a more chaotic way – for instance, by breaking a pot and counting the shards, which decrees the number of days/months/years the union will last.

Sex Magic for One

'To be comfortable in one's skin' is a phrase that the French use to describe someone who is not necessarily beautiful in any obvious way, but is none the less alluring. Everyone should be able to love themselves for what they are in spirit and body, without bowing to the constant bombardment of modern pressures to change and conform, or being weighted down by the baggage of destructive narcissistic self-worship.

This is doubly important when practising magic, as dissatisfactions, suppressions or delusions can easily be unleashed by the energies raised, making both spell and caster unstable and the results unpredictable. To be truly comfortable you must be able to be totally honest with yourself, knowing and accepting all parts, thus creating a totally beautiful, whole, sexy person.

There are many ways that the magical practitioner can begin to open themselves up to true self-knowledge, but one of the most widely used and effective is by studying the Eastern tradition of chakras. One of the more advanced techniques allows us to hone our meditation skills and learn about each type of energy used in magic. The first, or base, chakra concerns itself with basic sexual drives and energies, then as knowledge of each chakra is attained during meditation the energy grows, eventually allowing the sexual energies to flow around our body, heart and mind, and back down around to the base chakra. This particular flow or technique is called the kundalini energy flow and, according to the Eastern gurus, is the basis of all sex.

As has been previously discussed, the process of making a sigil or talisman can be completed and empowered by the addition of sexual energies and fluids, and these energies can always be heightened by use of Tantric methods or indeed favoured toys to increase the pleasurable energies of the solitary practitioner!

MIRROR MAGIC SPELL

❧❧

Another method of getting to know yourself is by using a mirror. We may have all gazed intently at our faces from time to time, but how well do we know the rest of our bodies, and is the physical body the only thing to be seen in the mirror?

This working is best done with plenty of time and no interruptions. First prepare your room as though you were expecting to entertain: clean and tidy up, light incense and candles, make up the bed with clean sheets and prop a mirror where you can see yourself in it from the pillow. Next prepare yourself as though you were going out on the town – a bath, perfume, make-up, outfit and perhaps even a glass of champagne.

Return to your room and lie on the bed. Then glance over at the mirror, and see yourself staring back. Take in the fix of your face, the tilt of your nose, the shade of your skin, the movement of your hair. Moving only your eyes, cover this familiar territory until you can close your eyes and still see your features. Start to cover the rest of your body – how are the arms held?

Do they support you? Can you see your waist? Do you bend at the knees? How do you position your feet? And so on.

Rise from the bed and remove one layer of clothing, then, returning to the same position on the bed, begin to let your eyes roam and see how you feel with one less layer. Do you feel exposed? Has your posture changed? Continue removing the layers, leaving as long as you can bear in between layers. Explore your physical presence along with your inner feelings. Do they reflect each other? Do you use clothing as disguise? When all the layers are removed try to remain in the same position as long as possible to enable you to overcome the usual urges to clothe and cover up, and to allow you the time to get to know the whole self. Do you still see the same you in those eyes in the mirror? Can you begin to see the magician within staring back?

When you feel the time is right, stand directly in front of the mirror, look into the eyes of the reflection and say, 'I love you.'

This sounds very easy right now, but you might not be able to manage it the first time, you might only manage a quick furtive glance and an 'I like you,' or you may say it and not mean it. Only you can tell, and only you can know how often you will need to repeat this exercise. Used wisely this is a very powerful tool for grounding yourself if you are feeling unsettled or troubled, as it will soon bring into focus any changes or imbalances within.

Sex Magic for More – from Orgy to Orgasm

LOVERS' BOWER

∂⌒✑

Here is a beautiful ritual for partners who wish to practise sex magic. It will create some amazing energies and is best enacted out of doors if a suitable place can be found.

You will need:

❖ *Rug and cushions*
(if outside)
❖ *Red roses or rose petals*
❖ *Picture of Aphrodite*
❖ *Red candles*
❖ *Rose incense*
❖ *Bowl of red wine*
❖ *Bowl of hot water (if outside)*
❖ *Rose oil*

109

To be done in a safe, secluded place in the light of the full moon.

Before sundown create a love bower. If you have been able to find a secluded spot, lay down a rug and some cushions to create a bed; this will form your altar. If you're at home you can use your own bed. Dress your altar bed with clean, sweet-smelling sheets, pillows and coverings. Adorn it with red roses or rose petals for passion. Hang an image of Aphrodite nearby. Place red candles and rose incense around the area or room, ready for lighting. Place a bowl of red wine at the foot of the bed. As the full moon rises, use warm water from a bowl to wash your lover gently. If you're at home, draw a ritual bath and scatter rose petals on the surface of the water, adding a few drops of rose oil. If possible, let the water catch the light of the full moon. Play some gentle and passionate music. Approach the altar bed together with your partner. Light the candles and incense, saying, 'We ignite the spirit of Aphrodite. Hail to thee, Goddess of Love!'

Undress each other slowly, by the candlelight and moonlight. Enter the bath and bathe each other in turn. As you wash each part of your lover's body, proclaim its beauty and sacredness.

Blessed by thy hair that caresses my face
Blessed by thine eyes that look upon me
with love
Blessed be thine ears that hear my
words of love
Blessed by thy lips that kiss
thy mouth that speaks to me of love
Blessed be thine arms that embrace
me in love
Blessed be thy heart that throbs in
the heat of love
Blessed be thy hands that touch me
Blessed be thy breast that contains
all sweetness
Blessed be thy belly that holds the
womb of life [for a woman]
Blessed be thy back that gladly
bears love's burdens

*Blessed be thy genitals that are the
gateway to mystery and ecstasy
Blessed be thy legs that carry thee to me
Blessed be thy feet that take
thee on love's journey.*

Kiss and wash each place as you name
it. As you emerge from the water,
chant together:

We are desire rebirthing.

Dry each other gently and place
flowing robes upon each other. Anoint
each other's brows with rose oil, saying:

Aphrodite bless you.

Walk hand in hand to the altar bed and
kneel before it. Raise up the bowl of wine
towards the image of Aphrodite, saying:

*Hail Goddess of Love,
who brought us together
We thank thee for thy wondrous gift of true
desire.*

*Bless our union tonight,
Give us openness that we may
flow into one another,
Strength to return to our separate selves,
And flexibility to dance and merge
and re-emerge again
May our love never be bound,
but fly in freedom
May our hearts never be cold,
but overflowing
With the heat of Thy love
So be it!
Blessed Be!*

Offer each other the wine. Rise and
embrace. Disrobe one another slowly.
Take each other's hands and slowly
move to the bed.

Where the magic goes now, the rest
is up to you...

This ritual or type of ritual can also be
cast with two or more partners, with
the idea to create a huge amount of
sexual energy connected with a single
aim, much like sets of batteries connect

together. If this is the desired ritual then it is usual for it to be conducted in the ceremony by one non-participant who will be the focus for all the energies raised and ultimately responsible for gathering and directing the magic at the appropriate moment.

Sex magic may involve actually having sex, and may not. As with the Great Rite, it can raise a vast amount of sexual energy but does not necessarily have to result in physical copulation. It is beneficial to know some of the techniques for non-coital sex magic, in case there ever comes a time when you are in a situation where you wish to partake in the Great Rite but your partner is not someone with whom you want to have sex. The following are techniques to build sexual energy:

★ Focused eye contact
★ Synchronized deep breathing
★ Touch, stroking
★ Circling around, holding hands
★ Anointing one another with scented oils
★ Teasing, retreat
★ Dancing, pelvic thrusting
★ Flagellation
★ Simulated sex
★ Fantasy visualisation

You can also perform the Great Rite or other sex magic purely symbolically, for example by inserting an athame, a god symbol, into a cup, a goddess symbol.

Goddess or vaginal symbols include:
★ Chalices
★ Cauldrons
★ Cups
★ Shells
★ Wine
★ Water
★ Menstrual blood
★ Soil
★ Salt

* The moon
* Crystal balls
* Lapis lazuli
* Rose quartz
* Circular or undulating motion

God or phallic
symbols include:
* Phallic-shaped
  figurines
* Athames
* Knives
* Swords
* Spades
* Wands or
  staves
* Candles
* Trees
* Bananas
* Dildos
* Cucumbers
* Thrusting or
  linear motion

Build Sexual Energy

113

Kinky!

Most magicians start on their path as a way of changing and developing themselves, a dissatisfaction with the status quo. This can mean a whole range of people are drawn to practising magic for many mundane reasons. However, they tend to find that magic becomes a release and form of free expression in the same way as art, music, literature or drama can transport someone to a different level of reality. When this journey of free expression is taken to its outer limits, it starts to address the very nature of one's personality and questions long-held personal and societal taboos.

Examining taboos can be helpful in confronting fears and long-held beliefs. A magician should aim to continue to grow and develop, though of course everyone is free to leave their taboos intact if they prefer. For some this can mean developing their eco-awareness beyond their usual recycling by getting involved in real protest for change in environmental abuses, thus overcoming a fear of stepping out of line; for others this can mean addressing polarities of gender and sexuality. Many magicians work to change the fixed ideas of 'normal', constructing creative new ways of living either theoretically or by example.

In sex magic, practitioners use these connections with taboo to heighten the creation of energies in much the same way as kinksters from the BDSM (Bondage & Discipline, Dominance & Submission, and S&M) scene raise their enjoyment by controlled use of kink and perversity. Of course, no one should be coerced to do anything they are not ready to do. That said, exploring your own system of sex magic should always be fun, demanding, fulfilling and effective, allowing yourself the best opportunity to be the person you should be.

'Every man and every woman is a star'
— Aleister Crowley, *Liber AL vel Legis*

Correspondence Tables

Chapter 7

Goddesses and Gods of Love and Sexuality

There are countless deities associated with love, fertility and sexuality in all their forms to be found in every culture throughout history. Here are some of the ones who you may want to work your sex magic with.

The Gods

Aizen Myo-O – Japanese
Amon – Egyptian
Amor – Roman
Cupid – Roman
Dionysus – Greek
Eros – Greek
Eueucoyotl – Aztec
Frey/Freyr – Norse
Ghede – Vodoun
Hymen – Greek/Roman
Kama – Hindu
Khem – Egyptian
Lempo – Finnish
Osiris – Egyptian
Pan – Greek
Peko – Estonian
Priapus – Greek
Quetzalcoatl – Aztec
Ratu-Mai-Mbula – Fijian
Rod – Slavic
Shiva – Hindu

The Goddesses

Achtland – Celtic
Anahita – Persian
Anna Perenna – Etruscan
Aphrodite – Greek
Benten – Japanese
Erzulie – Voodoo
Freya – Norse
Hathor – Egyptian
Havea lolo fonua – Polynesian
Hecate – Greek
Inanna – Sumerian
Ishtar – Assyrian
Isis – Egyptian
Lakshmi – Hindu
Luamerava – African
Mami Wata – African
Mens – Roman
Oshun Ana – African
Pacha Mama – Aztec
P'an Chin-lien – Chinese
Qadesh – Syrian

Thalia – Greek
Tlazolteot – Aztec
Ursule – Haitian
Ururupuin – Micronesian
Urvasi – Hindu
Var – Norse
Venus – Roman
Vesta – Roman
Voluptas – Roman
Xtabay – Mayan

Herbs

Here are a few herbs and spices, together with their corresponding magical properties, that you may want to use in your spells and combine together in your teas, baths, pillows and mojo bags. All these can be used in the state that they are most commonly found, whether dried, fresh, whole or powdered, but do consult a modern herbal encyclopaedia or herbalist before using anything new to you.

Herb	Planet	Element	Use
Adam and Eve Root	Venus	Water	These twinned roots are used to win the one you desire – the woman receives an Eve root, the man receives an Adam root. Married couples can exchange to confirm their fidelity.
Angelica Root	Sun	Fire	Angelica protects against negativity and fills its user with positive energy and joyfulness. If taken when pregnant it can cause miscarriage.
Balm of Gilead	Venus	Water	When carried about the person this will attract new love or help mend a broken heart.
Basil	Mars	Fire	Use in love spells. Place it on your sleeping lover to keep them true or put in the bath to wash away memories of an old love in order to let a new love in.

Bay Leaves	Sun	Fire	The bay leaf was used as incense or chewed by the priestesses at Delphi to help induce visions, clairvoyance and wisdom. It is often scattered or burned during exorcisms. Place under your pillow to bring lucid dreams or carry it about your person to ward off evil. Add to cleansing tea.
Black Coshosh	Mars	Earth	The root is carried to attract a lover or placed in the bedroom or bath for lust.
Cacao (Chocolate)	Venus	Water	Cacao was traditionally the Aztec's Food of the Gods. Can help with depression and dispels negativity. It is also an aphrodisiac and thus often used in sex magic. Also used when attempting to make contact with the spirit world.

Camomile	Sun	Water	Use in tea or incense to help relax mind and body and aid meditation. Use in ritual cleansing baths or splash on your face to help attract love.
Caraway	Mercury	Air	Acts as an aphrodisiac when used in cooking. Use in spells to ensure fidelity in your lover or attract a new one.
Cardamon	Venus	Water	A favourite of Erzulie, these seeds can be mulled in wine, added to sachets or burned in incense to promote lustful feelings.
Carob	Mars	Fire	Middle-Eastern pods often used as a chocolate substitute but, although the flavour is similar, the correspondences are opposite. Believed to induce lustful feelings as the tree blossoms give off a semen-like smell.

Catnip	Water	Venus	Used in magic relating to animals, such as healing pets. Enhances psychic abilities. Use as a tea to bring happiness and peace of mind. Can also be used during meditation. Useful in love magic when used with rose petals.
Cayenne Pepper	Mars	Fire	Used in love spells to represent the fieriness of the spirit. Like High John the Conqueror it will boost the effects of any spell.
Cedar	Sun	Fire	Can help attract new love when used in love spells. Carry in wallet to attract money. Burn as incense to enhance psychic powers.
Cinnamon	Sun	Fire	Cinnamon oil was used by both the ancient Egyptians and Romans in their temples. It is sacred to Venus and Aphrodite and is a powerful male aphrodisiac. Evokes spirituality, success, healing, psychic powers, lust, protection, love.

Clover, Red	Mercury	Air	An excellent fertility herb. Helps the process of moving on after a lost love to allow for new love to blossom. Aids in protection, money, love, fidelity, exorcism, success, clairvoyance and beauty magic. Brings good luck.
Cloves	Jupiter	Fire	Use as incense to attract money, purify, gain luck or stop gossip. Used in exorcism. Carry to attract a lover.
Cumin	Mars	Fire	Used in love spells to ensure fidelity. When soaked in wine the seeds act as an aphrodisiac. Place the seeds in close proximity to a treasured object to ensure it stays with you.

Damiana	Mars	Fire	Often used in sex magic, as it is a mild aphrodisiac. Use it to brew a seductive tea for you and your lover. When burned it enhances visions. Use caution with this herb.
Dandelion Leaf	Jupiter	Air	Use the root in a tea to enhance psychic ability or put under pillow for visionary dreams. Sacred to Hecate, Queen of Witches, so is often used in Samhain rituals. The herb has many healing and nutritional properties.
Dill	Mercury	Fire	Used to protect against harm, either hung over the entrance to the house or carried in a sachet about the person. Often used in love and sex magic. Add to the bath to attract the one you love.

Dragon's Blood (resin)	Mars	Fire	Used in incenses to increase potency and energy in all spells. Often burned to entice a lover home.
Fig	Jupiter	Fire	Often seen on Beltane altars. Sacred to Dionysus and Juno so is often used in fertility and love spells, particularly when sewn into mojo bags.
Flax Seed	Mercury	Fire	Often used in beauty spells. Bowls of seeds placed around the home will help maintain harmony within the house. Keep in wallet or purse to attract wealth. Eat seeds to get rid of depression. Very beneficial to health as helps fight cholesterol.
Galangal Root	Mars	Fire	Also known as Low John the Conqueror. Brings good luck and wealth. Carry or scatter in the bedroom to promote lust. Used to enhance psychic abilities. Often used in powdered form in incense to help dispel negative magic and curses.

Gardenia	Moon	Water	Use in incense to increase spirituality, love and peace or carry about the person to attract love.
Garlic	Mars	Fire	Garlic is sacred to Hecate and the ancient Greeks would place it on altars as an offering to her. It is the ultimate herb to use for protection against negative entities and infections. It has great healing and strengthening properties.
Ginger	Mars	Fire	Used in love spells and to promote success and power. Increases the potency of all spells when consumed before rituals.
Ginseng Powder	Sun	Fire	Used in love and sex magic to attract love and strengthen sexual potency. Also used in spells to draw wealth. Can be made into a tea which acts as an aphrodisiac. Has many beneficial properties when taken to improve and maintain health.

Hibiscus Flower	Venus	Water	The flowers can be used to make a tea which serves as an aphrodisiac and induces erotic dreams. Often used to enhance psychic ability and aid in divination. Acts as a relaxant.
Holly Leaf	Mars	Fire	Promotes good luck. Often used in dream magic. The wood of the Holly tree is often used to make magical tools as it adds power to your will and thus enhances spells.
Juniper Berries	Sun	Fire	Useful for protection magic, especially when used in incense form. It can also be burned or carried to attract healthy energy and love. Wear the dried berries as a necklace to attract a sexual partner.

Lavender	Mercury	Air	Lavender is used in a variety of ways to evoke love, protection, chastity, purification and peace. Roman soldiers used the oil to aid in healing. The fragrance is particularly pleasing to men.
Lime Tree Flowers (Linden)	Jupiter	Air	The flowers are made into a tea to promote relaxation and calm. When worn they offer protection, luck, longevity and help with sleep when mixed with lavender flowers.
Lotus Root	Moon	Water	The Lotus is used as an antidote to love spells and is a symbol of life mysteries and spirituality.
Mandrake Root	Mercury	Fire	Sacred to Hathor, goddess of love, and has long been used by witches and healers. It offers protection and attracts love, money, fertility and health. Mandrake is one of the roots that intensifies the power of any spell.

Morning Glory Blossoms	Neptune	Water	The flowers promote happiness and peace and help to induce visions when used as an incense. Place a sachet of the seeds under your pillow to stop nightmares and induce psychic dreams. Must not be consumed as they are toxic.
Moss	Jupiter	Earth	Use in prosperity spells and any magic concerning Mother Earth. For good luck, especially with money or the opposite sex, carry any type of moss removed from a graveyard.
Orris Root	Venus	Water	Used in powder form to draw love. Protects from evil spirits, particularly when hung in the house. Roots and leaves added to the bath are good for personal protection.

Passion Flower	Venus	Water	This flower is often used in love spells and as an aphrodisiac. It has calming properties and promotes peaceful sleep. Attracts friendship and wealth.
Patchouli	Saturn	Earth	This strong-scented and earthy plant is used as leaves in tea and burned as incense to evoke fertility and lust.
Raspberry Leaf	Venus	Water	Useful during pregnancy when prepared as a tea to ease the symptoms of nausea and vomiting. Has many healing properties, particularly with ailments relating to the kidneys. Offers calm, protection, healing and love.
Rose Hips	Venus	Water	The bead-like hips can be strung into a necklace to attract a lover. They contain many essential vitamins and if a woman eats them during her menstrual period they can replace depleted vitamins.

Rosemary	Sun	Fire	Rosemary incense has power to purify and cleanse and is also used in love and lust spells and potions. Use for healing, focus, youthfulness and protection.
Rose Petals	Venus	Water	Scatter petals around the home and bedroom when performing love spells and to promote domestic peace and happiness. Make into a tea and drink before bed for prophetic dreams.
Sage	Jupiter	Air	Has many purifying properties. Use in incense form during rituals to cleanse and bless all the nooks and crannies of your home to get rid of and guard against negative energies and influences. The smoke also aids with divination.

Salt	Saturn	Earth	Salt is used to purify and consecrate ritual tools. It can also be sprinkled around your sacred space to clear it of any negative influences. Can be dissolved in a bowl of water to symbolize the dissolving of evil.
Scullcap	Saturn	Water	Wearing this around the body protects your lover from temptations. Brings peace and harmony to the home.
Star Anise	Jupiter	Air	Used to help with meditation and increase psychic powers. Also a good ingredient to add to a purification bath. Put under pillow to stop bad dreams. Often used on altars to charge them with power. Can be carried as charms to attract good luck.

Tea	Sun	Fire	Tea leaves sewn into mojo bags or used in incenses will attract prosperity. Use as a stimulating base for all lust-inducing infusions. After drinking, the leaves can be used to scry. Green tea is extremely beneficial to health, being rich in antioxidants.
Thyme	Venus	Water	Used in spells and incense for healing and purification. Women who wear a sprig of the herb in their hair become irresistible to potential lovers. Can increase psychic powers when carried about the person.
Tobacco Leaf	Mars	Fire	Tobacco is sacred to Native Americans, who tie the leaves together in pieces of cloth and hang them around their ceremonial spaces. They believe that smoking tobacco helps them communicate with spirits. Can be used as sage is, in an incense which is used to purify the home.

Valerian Root	Venus	Water	This herb can be used to purify a ritual space when burned. When drunk as a tea it is a powerful relaxant and tranquilizer, so is useful for dream magic and in ritual baths. Women wearing the root will gain many admirers and couples who grow or keep it in the home or garden will live in harmony with each other.
Vanilla	Venus	Water	Vanilla-scented sugar is used to 'sweeten' love sachets and can be used in food to induce lust. Vanilla oil can be worn to promote lustful feelings.
Violet	Venus	Water	When mixed with lavender and worn or burned in incense violets are a powerful sexual stimulant.

White Willow	Moon	Water	The leaves, bark and wood have many uses, particularly in healing and protection spells. Spirits can be summoned by burning with sandalwood. Carry the leaves to attract love and use the wood to fashion wands.
Yarrow Flower	Venus	Water	Use to adorn the home or carry in a sachet or amulet to ensure a lasting union with your lover. Has many healing properties and is particularly good for colds.

Colours

Colours play a powerful role in witchcraft and magic. They are carefully considered and assigned to many aspects of spell-making, ritual magic and the celebration of the festivals.

Colour correspondences are used to represent the influences of deities, planets, moods, the zodiac or time, but are also widely used in meditation and visualization techniques, as colours have symbolic associations representing their own frequencies that bestow specific influences.

For example, the energy centres in the body known to Eastern teachings as chakras are each assigned a colour to aid in the representation of the chakra and its properties, and also to enable easy meditation. Colour lends a different and distinct character to each.

Colour	Planet	Description
White	Moon	Contains all colours, so can be used as a replacement for any other colour. It symbolizes purity of spirit. White altar candles represent this spirit in all its forms, whether that be elemental, angelic or otherwise. Used to help attune with the Goddess and for purification of any kind. Helps with divination and clairvoyance.
Silver	Moon and Mercury	The colour of wisdom, communication and healing. Also associated with the Goddess, feminine cycles and mysteries, psychic development, lunar magic, occult knowledge and intuition.
Grey	Pluto	The most neutral colour so is used to represent cancellation, neutrality, vision quests and travels to the Other World.
Turquoise	Mercury	Represents intellectual and intuitive insights, creativity and originality, devotional or spiritual renewal and harmony between partners.
Blue	Jupiter	Used to evoke the power of Jupiter. Blue is a Goddess colour and the colour most associated with the elements of water and air. Used to attune to the oceanic Goddesses. Used in matters relating to wealth and abundance, truth and justice, joy, opportunity, healing, loyalty and prophecy.
Indigo	Saturn	Indigo is the colour of inertia and is used to stop certain situations or people. Use in rituals that require a deep meditational state. It can also be used to influence such matters as binding, patience, stability, neutralization, material gain and protection.

Violet	Moon	Represents justice, royalty, meditation, idealism, mysticism, religion and guidance. Its magical uses include protection, power, spirit contact, divination, spiritual and psychic powers and astral projection. The colour is also used in magic to break curses and combat negativity.
Purple	Mercury	Evokes the power of Mercury and influences occult and hidden aspects. Used by those who work with pure divine power (magicians, priests and priestesses) and those who wish to deepen their spiritual awareness of the God and Goddess. Aids meditation and psychic abilities.
Lavender	Mercury	Helps with spiritual development, psychic growth and divination. Promotes inner peace and sensitivity to the Other World. Use it to help you when seeking answers to difficult questions or favours from the deities or spirits.
Pink	Venus	Represents the realm of Venus and the associated qualities of friendship, love and harmony. Used to enhance spellwork for romance, emotional love, caring, partnerships and healing.
Red	Mars	The colour of passion, vigour, sex, vitality, lust, power, strength, motivation and courage. It represents the God and all things male and is the most appropriate colour to use in sexual magic.
Brown	Earth	Helps to evoke qualities such as grounding and stability. Used to protect the home, people and animals. Symbolic of strength and endurance, aids in improving concentration and helps to create a link to the animal realms.

Orange	Jupiter	Represents the God and can be a substitute for red when evoking solar energies. Can be used to amplify the effects of other colours, but is also used in such matters as health, life changes, strength, luck, success, celebration and business and legal affairs.
Gold	Sun	Represents the power of the Sun and all the solar deities and masculine energy. It evokes inner strength, confidence, power, success and self-realization.
Yellow	Sun	Also used to evoke the energies of the sun, but the full fiery strength is tempered to allow for healing, change, vitality, communication, happiness, harmony and joy.
Green	Venus and Mercury	Represents the male and feminine deities. Used to evoke nature, fertility, growth, abundance, healing, marriage, prosperity and balance.
Black	Pluto	Used to symbolize the deities of the Underworld, outer space and the absence of all colour. Blackness is the source of all things, divine energy and life. Black is used when working with stability, patience, protection, the birth/death cycle, obstacles and addictions.

Trees

There is a special and sacred place for trees in the belief systems of the world, as from the first stirrings of society they have been seen as being the connection between all that is in this world and in the other. Nearly every religion and tradition has a strand of lore dedicated to a tree – a tree of life, for instance, whose roots reaching into the Underworld exactly mirror the branches reaching into the heavens.

The Underworld, as symbol of the God, was connected to the heavens, home of the Goddess, with the tree as the link between the two realms. This gave rise to the dictum 'as above, so below'.

Nature spirits and elementals are also believed to dwell in trees; normally indisposed to helping humans, they could under certain circumstances be petitioned to aid in magic and to communicate with deities. Offerings to petition or praise were often made to the spirits or gods at these sacred sites and are still placed by modern pagans in honour of these sacred trees.

The Twelve Main Trees

Alder	The Alder is associated with courage and it represents the evolving spirit.
Ash	In Celtic mythology the Ash is known as the tree of enchantment and it is said that the Welsh magician Gwydion fashioned his wands from ash wood.
Birch	The Birch tree represents the rebirth of the Sun from winter's solstice. Both the Birch and the Elder stand on either side of the one Nameless day (the day in-between the end of a year and the beginning of the new one). They both represent a link between life and death, with the Birch being the birth of new life.
Elder	The symbol of both death and rebirth. Like the Winter Solstice, it highlights a time of evolution. The Celts believed that it was during this time that their sun or solar spirit was held prisoner. It is also a time of trouble and struggle for supremacy.
Hawthorn	The Hawthorn is associated with the sacred and the unlucky; it is especially unlucky to destroy it. It symbolizes the Chalice, as it too represents divine secrets and everlasting life.
Hazel	The nut of this tree is the emblem of concentrated wisdom. It was thought one could gain knowledge just by eating hazelnuts. In this aspect it is associated with the Salmon, a sacred symbol of wisdom.
Holly	A symbol of luck and good fortune. In Celtic mythology the Holly is the evergreen twin of the Oak. The Oak rules the light part of the year while the Holly rules the dark part, and represents the evergreen aspects of earth.

Ivy	In contrast to the Vine, Ivy is evergreen, and it represents the perennial aspects of the human psyche. The Celts associated Ivy with their lunar goddess Arianrhod and the dark side of the moon. Ivy represents the mysterious and the mystical.
Oak	The principal sacred tree of the Druids, the Oak symbolized the turning of the year. It represents the trial we all go through in life as we develop into whom we are meant to be. It stands for change, sacrifice and understanding.
Rowan	The Rowan (or Mountain Ash) was believed to be a magical tree and its red berries the food of the gods.
Vine	The Vine is the symbol of sensuality and emotions, and also represents the Autumn Equinox, that moment of balance when light and dark hold equal positions, just before light surrenders its hold to darkness. To the Celtic mind it represented the balance of the mundane and the supernatural; the mortal and the immortal.
Willow	The Willow has since ancient times always been associated with death. It is considered to be a tree of enchantment, and is associated with Hecate, Queen of the Underworld.

Time

The earliest clocks and calendars, such as Stonehenge, measured fixed points of the day, night and year. But as people became more sophisticated, cultures such as the Sumerians, Mayans, Chinese and Egyptians developed sundials, water-clocks and other methods to measure the hours, using the travel of the celestial bodies day and night. In Europe, during most of the Middle Ages (roughly 500 CE to 1500 CE), technological advancement virtually ceased. Sundial styles evolved, but didn't move far from ancient Egyptian principles until the invention of the pendulum and clockwork timepieces with the regular 12-hour divisions we are more familiar with today.

Before 2000 BCE, the Babylonians used a year of 12 alternating 29-day and 30-day lunar months, giving a 354-day year. In contrast, the Mayans of Central America relied not only on the Sun and Moon, but also on the planet Venus, to establish 260-day and 365-day calendars.

If you or your spell call for the need to be as precise as possible, it is best to align your magical workings with the most appropriate correspondences, timing being one of the most basic. Magical time works in the way that most cultures used before the Common Era, splitting the day and night each into 12 equal parts.

The *merkhet*, the oldest-known astronomical tool, was an Egyptian development of around 600 BCE. A pair of *merkhets* were used to establish a north-south line (or meridian) by aligning them with the Pole Star. They could then be used to mark off night-time hours by determining when certain other stars crossed the meridian.

To calculate the magical or planetary hour of the day or night which is most auspicious, you first need to determine the point of sunrise and sunset, calculate the amount of minutes between these two times and divide that by 12. Each planetary hour will last that many minutes, with the first hour beginning precisely at sunrise and corresponding with the ruling planet of the day. You can now choose the appropriate time for your spell or working according to the following tables.

Sunday is ruled by the **Sun**

Monday is ruled by the **Moon**

Tuesday is ruled by **Mars**

Wednesday is ruled by **Mercury**

Thursday is ruled by **Jupiter**

Friday is ruled by **Venus**

Saturday is ruled by **Saturn**

Planetary Hours of the Day (sunrise to sunset)

	1	2	3	4	5	6
Sunday	Sun	Venus	Mercury	Moon	Saturn	Jupiter
Monday	Moon	Saturn	Jupiter	Mars	Sun	Venus
Tuesday	Mars	Sun	Venus	Mercury	Moon	Saturn
Wednesday	Mercury	Moon	Saturn	Jupiter	Mars	Sun
Thursday	Jupiter	Mars	Sun	Venus	Mercury	Moon
Friday	Venus	Mercury	Moon	Saturn	Jupiter	Mars
Saturday	Saturn	Jupiter	Mars	Sun	Venus	Mercury

	7	8	9	10	11	12
Sunday	Mars	Sun	Venus	Mercury	Moon	Saturn
Monday	Mercury	Moon	Saturn	Jupiter	Mars	Sun
Tuesday	Jupiter	Mars	Sun	Venus	Mercury	Moon
Wednesday	Venus	Mercury	Moon	Saturn	Jupiter	Mars
Thursday	Saturn	Jupiter	Mars	Sun	Venus	Mercury
Friday	Sun	Venus	Mercury	Moon	Saturn	Jupiter
Saturday	Moon	Saturn	Jupiter	Mars	Sun	Venus

Planetary Hours of the Night (sunset to sunrise)

	1	2	3	4	5	6
Sunday	Jupiter	Mars	Sun	Venus	Mercury	Moon
Monday	Venus	Mercury	Moon	Saturn	Jupiter	Mars
Tuesday	Saturn	Jupiter	Mars	Sun	Venus	Mercury
Wednesday	Sun	Venus	Mercury	Moon	Saturn	Jupiter
Thursday	Moon	Saturn	Jupiter	Mars	Sun	Venus
Friday	Mars	Sun	Venus	Mercury	Moon	Saturn
Saturday	Mercury	Moon	Saturn	Jupiter	Mars	Sun

	7	8	9	10	11	12
Sunday	Saturn	Jupiter	Mars	Sun	Venus	Mercury
Monday	Sun	Venus	Mercury	Moon	Saturn	Jupiter
Tuesday	Moon	Saturn	Jupiter	Mars	Sun	Venus
Wednesday	Mars	Sun	Venus	Mercury	Moon	Saturn
Thursday	Mercury	Moon	Saturn	Jupiter	Mars	Sun
Friday	Jupiter	Mars	Sun	Venus	Mercury	Moon
Saturday	Venus	Mercury	Moon	Saturn	Jupiter	Mars

According to the ancient grimoire, *The Greater Key of Solomon*, each of the planets have the following properties:

In the Days and Hours of Saturn

thou canst perform experiments to summon the Souls from Hades, but only of those who have died a natural death. Similarly on these days and hours thou canst operate to bring either good or bad fortune to buildings; to have familiar Spirits attend thee in sleep; to cause good or ill success to business, possessions, goods, seeds, fruits, and similar things, in order to acquire learning; to bring destruction and to give death, and to sow hatred and discord.

The Days and Hours of Jupiter

are proper for obtaining honours, acquiring riches; contracting friendships, preserving health; and arriving at all that thou canst desire.

148

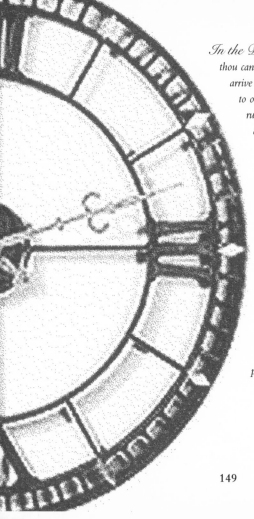

In the Days and Hours of Mars

thou canst make experiments regarding War; to arrive at military honour; to acquire courage; to overthrow enemies; and further to cause ruin, slaughter, cruelty, discord; to wound and to give death.

The Days and Hours of the Sun

are very good for perfecting experiments regarding temporal wealth, hope, gain, fortune, divination, the favour of princes; to dissolve hostile feeling, and to make friends.

The Days and Hours of Venus

are good for forming friendships; for kindness and love; for joyous and pleasant undertakings, and for travelling.

149

The Days and Hours of Mercury
are good to operate for eloquence and
intelligence; promptitude in business; science
and divination; wonders; apparitions; and
answers regarding the future. Thou canst also
operate under this Planet for thefts; writings;
deceit; and merchandise.

The Days and Hours of the Moon
are good for embassies; voyages, envoys;
messages; navigation; reconciliation; love; and
the acquisition of merchandise by water.

*The Hours of the Sun, of Jupiter,
and of Venus,* are adapted for preparing
any operations whatsoever of love, of
kindness…

Depending on how you follow or
formulate your favourite sex spells, all
of the planetary days and hours can
have their uses, with the Venusian ones
having special relevance.

Planets and Astrology

In the universe there exists power to be tapped, and certain entities to aid you in your aims. We can call them gods, spirits, watchers and angels; or depersonalize them as powers or forces. However, once their help has been enlisted they are as dependent on us as we are on them, so be honest and courteous. The elemental power tides of the universe are marked by the movement of the stars; though they are not the sources of power themselves, they can be seen as the main indicators of its ebb and flow.

Sun

Throughout the year the Sun journeys through the heavens, passing in turn through each astrological sign. As it does so it makes various angles (or aspects) with other planets, which give us insight into the relationships and areas of our lives which will be affected at any one time. Finding the right time to do your spell can make all the difference!

Moon – Phases

Every month the Moon goes through a whole cycle from Full Moon, Last Quarter, New Moon and First Quarter. The phases are most important for your magic as spells cast to grow or increase things are generally done from the New or Dark Moon period until the Full Moon, and the spells cast to remove or decrease things are then generally done from the Full Moon to the New Moon. This cycle is also reflected in the way we think about the Goddess as maiden, mother and crone.

Mercury – the planet of mind and communication

Venus – the planet of harmony, grace and love

Mars – the planet of energy, passion and courage

Jupiter – the planet of luck, wealth, health and joy

Saturn – the planet of reason and order, time and old age

Uranus – the planet of intuition, unexpected change and originality

Neptune – the planet of dreams, illusion, escapism and divination

Pluto – the planet of finality and death, part of the cycle before rebirth

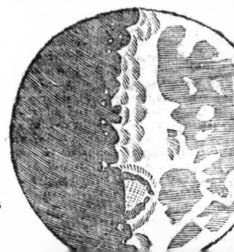

Seasons

The cycle of the year is marked by modern pagans with eight main festivals which are also particularly potent times for magic, each with its own characteristics and flavour. Against the eternal life of the Goddess these festivals mark the short life of mankind, through birth, growth, decline and death during the course of the year.

The wheel of the year

Samhain - October
Yule - Winter Solstice - December
Imbolc - Candlemass - February
Oestara - Spring Equinox - March
Beltane/Walpurgisnacht - May
Litha - Summer Solstice - June
Lammas/Lughnasadh - August
Hellith's Day/Mabon - Autumn
Equinox - September

The earliest Egyptian calendar was based on the Moon's cycles, but later the Egyptians realised that the 'Dog Star' in Canis Major, which we call Sirius, rose next to the Sun every 365 days, about when the annual inundation of the Nile began. Based on this knowledge, they devised a 365-day calendar that seems to have begun around 3100 BCE, which thus seems to be one of the earliest years, as we know them, recorded in history.

Bibliography and Recommended Reading

- Anand, Margo, *The Art of Sexual Ecstacy*, Thorsons, 1992
- Antelme, Ruth Schulman, & Rossini, Stéphane, *Sacred Sexuality in Ancient Egypt*, Inner Traditions, 2001
- Armour, Robert A., *Gods and Myths of Ancient Egypt*, American University in Cairo Press, 1986
- Bird, Stephanie Rose, *Sticks, Stones, Roots & Bones*, Llewelyn, 2004
- Canizares, Raul, *The Life and Works of Marie Laveau*, Original Publications, 2001
- Culpeper, Nicholas, *Colour Herbal*, Foulsham, 2002
- Culpeper, Nicholas, *Complete Herbal*, Wordsworth, 1995
- Cunningham, Scott, *Encyclopedia of Magical Herbs*, Llewelyn, 2003
- Cunningham, Scott, *The Complete Book of Incense, Oils & Brews*, Llewelyn, 2003
- Drury, Nevill, *DonJuan, Mescalito and Modern Magic*, Arkana, 1985
- Dunwich, Gerina, *Exploring Spellcraft*, New Page Books, 2001
- DuQuette, Lon Milo & Hyatt, Christopher S. , *Aleister Crowley's Illustrated Geotia*, New Falcon, 2004
- Durdin-Robertson, *The Year of the Goddess*, Aquarian, 1990
- Eason, Cassandra, *Ancient Egyptian Magic*, Vega, 2003
- Feuerstein, Georg, *Sacred Sexuality*, Inner Traditions, 2003
- Frater U. D., *Secrets of Western Sex Magic*, Llewelyn 2001
- Green, Miranda, *Celtic Godesses*, British Museum Press, 1995
- Grimassi, Raven, *The Witches' Craft*, Llewelyn, 2002
- Hare, J. B., *The Internet Sacred Text Archive*, CD ROM, 2004
- Kaldera, Raven & Schartzstein, Tannin, *The Urban Primitive*, Llewelyn, 2002
- King, Frances, *Sexuality, Magic and Perversion*, Feral House 2002
- Knight, Sirona & Telesco, Patricia, *The Cyber Spellbook*, New Page, 2002

- Lamond, Frederic, *Fifty Years of Wicca*, Green Magic 2004
- McCrickard, Janet, *Incense*, Quest Magazine, 1995
- Miller, Richard Alan, *The Magical and Ritual Use of Herbs*, Destiny Books, 1983
- Parrinder, Geoffrey, *Witchcraft: European and African*, Faber, 1958
- Paterson, Jacqeline Memory, *Tree Wisdom*, Thorsons, 1996
- Penczak, Christopher, *City Magick*, Weiser, 2001
- Roberts, Alison, *Hathor Rising*, Northgate, 2001
- Schultes, Richard Evans & Hofmann, Albert, *Plants of the Gods*, Healing Arts Press, 1992
- Sharif, Keti, *Bellydance*, Allen & Unwin, 2004
- Telesco, Patricia, *Kitchen Witch's Guide to Divination*, New Page, 2004
- West, Kate, *The Real Witches' Kitchen*, Element, 2002
- Wilson, Robert Anton, *Sex, Drugs and Magic*, New Falcon, 2000

- John M. Riddle, *Contraception and Abortion from the Ancient World to the Renaissance*, Cambridge, MA: Harvard University Press, 1992.

www.omorganics.com
www.iamshaman.com
www.geocities.com/soho/lofts/2938/magic6knots.html
www.rotten.com
www.luckymojo.com
www.wikipedia.org
www.hort.purdue.edu/newcrop/morton/bael_fruit.html
http://realmagick.com
www.natradisiacs.com
www.khakani.com/freemagicspells
www.goddessherself.com
www.wuzzle.org/cave/lovegods.html
www.wejees.net/herbs.html
www.godchecker.com
www.thekeep.org/~kunoichi/kunoichi/themestream/sexuality.html

Stockists

- Treadwells Bookshop
  34 Tavistock Street, Covent Garden,
  London, WC2E 7PB (UK)
  Tel: 020 7240 8906
  www.treadwells-london.com
- New Aeon Books
  95 Oldham Street,
  Manchester, M4 1LW(UK)
  Tel: 0161 839 9293
  www.newaeonbooks.co.uk
- Mystic Fragrance & Medicinal Herbs
  145b Stoke Newington Rd,
  London, N16 8BP (UK)
  Tel: 020 7254 4776
- Watkins Esoteric Centre & Bookshop
  13–19 Cecil Court,
  London, WC2N 4EZ (UK)
  Tel: 020 7863 2182
  www.watkinsbooks.com
- Natural Fragrance Co
  224 Holloway Rd,
  London, N7 8DA (UK)
  Tel: 020 7607 1986

British internet suppliers

www.wyrdshop.com
www.themooncup.co.uk
www.magickrose.co.uk
www.peacockangel.com

American internet suppliers

www.witchway.net/books/read.html
www.luckymojo.com
www.neworleansmistic.com
www.celestialwicca.com
www.ravensflight.net
www.abaxion.com
www.botelegua.com/Merchant2/
merchant.mvc

Australian internet suppliers

www.whitemagic.com.au/products.html
www.witchesworkshop.com/links/
australian_egroups.html
www.ozpagan.com/mainindx.html

Index